The
Easy Vegan

OVER 440 DELICIOUS RECIPES
AND MENUS FOR EVERY
DAY OF THE YEAR

JANET HUDSON

HAMPTON ROADS

D1410205

For Tom

remembering all the good food and

'taste tests' that got us to where we are today

First U.S. edition published in 2012 by
Hampton Roads Publishing Company, Inc.,
Charlottesville VA 22906
www.redwheelweiser.com

Published by arrangement with
HarperCollins*Publishers* Ltd

First published by Thorsons 2005

© Janet Hudson 2012

ISBN 978-1-57174-676-4

Printed and bound in Great Britain by
Clays Ltd, St Ives plc

MIX
Paper from
responsible sources
FSC **FSC™ C007454**
www.fsc.org

FSC™ is a non-profit international organisation established to promote
the responsible management of the world's forests. Products carrying the
FSC label are independently certified to assure consumers that they come
from forests that are managed to meet the social, economic and
ecological needs of present or future generations,
and other controlled sources.

Find out more about HarperCollins and the environment at
www.harpercollins.co.uk/green

Contents

The Easy Vegan: Hindsight is 100%

It was no more than a few years ago, and it still occurs occasionally today, that people frequently commented, "Vegan, that is a hard diet to follow!" or "... being vegan, that is so bland!" And, I must admit, back then following a vegan diet was bland and a bit boring. A couple of lettuce leaves, a radish, and a slice of tomato, or a cup of oatmeal might have been it (just ask my husband who lived on salad and oatmeal for months). In order to evolve, I had to think outside the box.

Just a short time prior to this I remember thinking, "Vegan-me? Vegetarian yes, but certainly not vegan." However, I was in search of an alternative to the "animal diet"—and because I was looking for the perfect lifestyle as well the perfect cuisine, it soon became clear that going vegan was the answer.

Some people choose this path in order to eat for better health—to feel good. Other vegetarians go vegan to show their concern and support for animal welfare. A plant-based diet is a responsible way of eating; it's the diet best suited to proper human nutrition. The plight of the world's hungry and the destruction of our natural resources remains a cause for others. In addition, the vegan diet, quite simply, is less costly.

My evolution as a vegan became my mantra, and a sort of spiritual realization. I remembered the comfort foods of my childhood and wished to combine those tastes while on my quest for perfect vegan fare.

The Easy Vegan is a sensory feast of fusion creations from my "out-of-the-box" experience: Light, cool salads mixing exotic greens such as watercress; refreshing tangy-tender leaves bathed in lime vinaigrette and tossed with jicima and avocado; hardy soups like Albondigas—flavor-packed with mildly-spiced veggie meatballs, brown rice, green chilies, zesty mint seasoning, and fresh vegetables. Ethnic entrees and sandwiches feature, too, including the Tempeh Reuben—smoked tempeh, red onion, mushroom, almond cheese, and sauerkraut with a Russian dressing; and "Shrimp" Curry, with freshly-harvested green beans and baby wax beans. And then there are the temptations—all natural, all vegan Apple Crisp, Tofu Cheesecake, Chai Tiramisu, Pumpkin Pecan Pie … and the smoothies and shakes—fresh, fresh, fresh!

As with any recipe book, more experienced cooks may want to modify some dishes according to desire—by adding more liquid for thinner consistency, cooking longer for softer vegetables etc. Try, adapt, and above all enjoy.

The EASY Vegan … Why did I wait so long? Hindsight is 100%!

Welcome Fellow Vegans!

I recall one visit to my folks' home shortly after I "graduated" to vegan. My father, the original carnivore, held up a fat juicy flank steak on his fork and commented how much I was missing out … in between a huge bite of mashed potatoes, butter dripping off his chin.

I knew then that they were the ones who were really missing out. Vegan is delicious, exotic, spicy, delicate foods full of flavor and robust tastes: and best of all it is the healthiest food that there is! Vegan dining is fun!

Beginning purely by experiment—mostly on friends and relatives—I began my mission to "convert" the non-believers. I started small, substituting my mother-in-law's cream (in her coffee) with almond milk and her butter with vegetable margarine. Often the switch was a success.

Searching for the best in vegan foods and creating vegan recipes for my family to enjoy became my passion. I discovered that humans unconsciously relate certain textures, shapes and consistencies in foods with taste ... and that those taste memories are associated with pleasant eating experiences.

I embarked on a journey—catering and cooking vegan. Packed lunches, buffet dinners and hors d'oeuvre parties—what great fun indeed! During one event—a birthday party—I served a "Beef" Burgundy Fondue dish. A gentleman kept pacing back and forth from the buffet to the kitchen. Finally, he blurted out:

"Where did you purchase your sirloin—Gelsons or Bristol Farms? This is the most tender beef that I have had in quite some time!"

I had prepared the dish with mushrooms.

Enough said. May I present to you this—a vegan feast, 365 days of the year!

Enjoy!

Janet

Hors d'oeuvres:

HOT AND COLD MINI ENTREES

Appetizers make for great

conversation ... these whet the

appetite for the entrée or satisfy

the soul as a meal on their own

Anaheim Poppers

Serves 12-24

24	anaheim peppers, washed
1 cup	chunky peanut or macadamia butter
½ quantity	Haute Mango Salsa recipe (page 328)

Place the peppers under a broiler or on an open flame and roast until the skins blister. Place the peppers in a plastic bag and fill with ice water. When the skins begin to peel off, remove them from the bag and peel the skins off (wearing gloves). Halve the peppers and remove the seeds.

Mix the butter and salsa and stuff the peppers with the mixture.

Artichoke Heart Muffins

Serves 24

24	wonton wrappers
12 ounces	artichoke hearts
¼ cup	finely diced red bell pepper
¼ cup	black olives, diced
2	garlic cloves, minced
½ cup	veggie parmesan shreds
½ cup	vegan mayonnaise dressing

Preheat the oven to 350°F.

Oil enough muffin pans for the 24 wrappers and place a wonton wrapper in each cup. Combine the remaining ingredients and spoon the mixture into the cups. Pinch each wrapper closed. Bake for 10–12 minutes. Serve warm.

Asparagus Surprise

Serves 6

6 slices	whole-wheat bread, crusts removed
12 tablespoons	vegetable margarine
6 dashes	powdered vegetable seasoning
6 tablespoons	soy cream cheese
6	parboiled asparagus spears
6 teaspoons	grated veggie parmesan

Preheat the oven to 325°F.

Lay out the bread slices and spread with ½ tablespoon of vegetable margarine on each slice, followed by a dash of vegetable seasoning and 1 tablespoon soy cream cheese.

Place an asparagus spear at the end of bread slice and roll up. Melt the remaining margarine, roll each slice in it and then roll them in the grated parmesan. Heat in the oven for 12 minutes, or until browned.

Asparagus with Sun-Dried Tomato Timbale

Makes 2 timbales

1 cup	fresh asparagus
Juice of 1	lemon
2 ounces	firm tofu
3 ounces	veggie cream cheese
Dash of	powdered vegetable seasoning
	salt and pepper to taste
¼ cup	minced scallions
1	garlic clove, minced
¼ cup	diced sun-dried tomatoes
¼ cup	veggie parmesan shreds
2 tablespoons	minced parsley
2	cherry tomatoes

Steam the asparagus then sprinkle it with the lemon juice. Reserve two tips and puree the remaining asparagus in a processor. Cool.

Combine the tofu and "cream cheese." Season with the vegetable powder, add salt and pepper to taste, and whip until smooth. Fold in the scallions and garlic then add the sun-dried tomatoes. Combine the veggie parmesan and parsley in a separate bowl.

Now assemble the dish. Spray two 3–4-inch molds with non-dairy vegetable spray. Line with plastic wrap and build up layers: first the veggie cream cheese mixture, then the parmesan mixture, then the asparagus; now repeat the layers.

Refrigerate 2 hours or, for best results, overnight. Unmold. Garnish with cherry tomato and an asparagus tip. Serve with veggies or toast.

Beau Monde Nibbles

Serves 8–12

2½ cups	vegan mayonnaise dressing
2 cups	veggie sour cream
4 teaspoons	Spice Islands Beau Monde seasoning
4 tablespoons	minced onion
4 tablespoons	chopped fresh parsley
2 teaspoons	fresh dill weed
6 ounces	veggie beef or pork, very finely chopped
1	round rye loaf

Mix all the ingredients, except the loaf, and let the mixture sit 8 hours or overnight.

Hollow out the loaf and cube the bread. If you wish, you can toast the cubes in a 275°F oven until browned.

Fill the loaf with the dip just before serving and serve with the cubed bread.

Beer-Battered Artichoke Hearts

Serves 4

¼ cup	oat milk
1 cup	whole-wheat flour
3 teaspoons	egg replacer
1 teaspoon	sea salt
½ cup	organic beer
2 cups	artichoke hearts, parboiled
	safflower oil

Puree the first four ingredients. Once the batter is smooth, stir in the beer.

Dip the artichokes into the batter and fry in safflower oil until brown and crispy.

These are good served with vegan mayonnaise dressing and lemon wedges.

Bruschetta

Serves 10

½ cup	olive oil
¼ cup	tomatillos or bell pepper, finely diced
¼ cup	finely diced white onion
2 teaspoons	chopped fresh basil
2 cups	vine-ripened tomatoes, finely diced
4 tablespoons	red wine
½ teaspoon	black pepper
1	baguette, cut into 1-inch slices

Preheat the oven to 275°F.

Coat a skillet with 2 teaspoons of olive oil. Place the tomatillos or peppers, onions, and basil in skillet; sauté for 2 minutes. Add the tomatoes, red wine, and pepper. Cook an additional 2 minutes. Remove from heat.

Place the baguette slices on a cookie sheet and brush with the remaining olive oil. Mound 2 tablespoons of tomato sauce on each baguette. Bake 4 minutes, or until crispy.

The following recipe expands on this theme, adding a few special ingredients to make it extra tasty.

Bravo! Bravo! Bruschetta

Serves 10

¼ cup	olive oil
¼ cup	finely diced bell pepper
¼ cup	finely diced white onion
2	ears corn, cut off stalk and parboiled
2 teaspoons	chopped fresh basil
2 cups	diced vine-ripened tomatoes
4 tablespoons	red wine
1	baguette, cut into 1-inch slices
1 teaspoon	black pepper
1 can	artichoke hearts or 6 fresh, prepared and diced
¼ cup	grated veggie parmesan

Preheat the oven to 275°F.

Coat a skillet with 2 teaspoons of olive oil. Place the peppers, onions, corn, and basil in the skillet; sauté for 2 minutes. Add the tomatoes and red wine. Cook an additional 2 minutes then remove from the heat.

Place the baguette slices on a cookie sheet and brush with the remaining olive oil. Mound 2 tablespoons of tomato sauce on each baguette. Top each slice with some artichoke and sprinkle with veggie cheese. Bake 4 minutes, or until crispy.

"California Dream'n" Shrimp Cocktail

Serves 4

Cocktail:

1 pound	veggie prawns, each cut into three pieces
1 cup	radish sprouts
2	Haas avocados
1	pink grapefruit, peeled and sectioned
1	white grapefruit, peeled and sectioned
2 cups	baby spinach
2 tablespoons	limejuice
¼ cup	toasted pine nuts

Dressing:

½ cup	grapefruit juice
3 tablespoons	limejuice
3 tablespoons	olive oil
¼ teaspoon	grated ginger root

Place all the cocktail ingredients in a bowl and toss. Place all the dressing ingredients in a screw-top jar or bottle. Shake and then pour the dressing over the salad.

Spoon into chilled sherbet dishes. Start dream'n.

Caponata Debut

Yields 4 cups

1	large eggplant, diced into cubes
1¾ teaspoons	sea salt
6 tablespoons	olive oil
1 cup	thinly sliced scallions, including greens (about two bunches)
2 tablespoons	chopped garlic
1 cup	diced celery, parboiled
½ teaspoon	red-pepper flakes
2½ cups	diced fresh tomatoes (6–8 medium)
6 tablespoons	chopped fresh basil
¼ cup	capers
6 ounces	(about ¾ cup) Greek olives, halved
½ teaspoon	cocoa powder
3 tablespoons	balsamic vinegar
1 tablespoon	maple syrup

Preheat the oven to 450°F.

Lay the eggplant on an aluminum foil-covered cookie sheet. Sprinkle ½ teaspoon salt over the eggplant and cover with another piece of aluminum foil. Place a weight on top and allow it to drain 15 minutes. Place 3 tablespoons of olive oil in skillet and heat for 2 minutes. Add the eggplant and cook for 6 minutes, stirring occasionally. Return the eggplant to the cookie sheet, sprinkle with ½ teaspoon salt and bake for 5 minutes. Cool.

Wipe the skillet and add the remaining 3 tablespoons of oil; heat for 2 minutes. Add the onions and sauté for 4 minutes. Add garlic, celery, red-pepper flakes, ¼ teaspoon salt; cook an additional 4 minutes. Add tomatoes, basil, eggplant, capers and olives; cook 6 minutes, bringing to a boil. Add the cocoa powder, mix well, and simmer 2 minutes. Heat vinegar and syrup until thickened, about 2 minutes. Add this to the vegetable mixture and stir. Simmer on low for 4 minutes. Remove from heat, cover, and refrigerate at least overnight (48 hours is best). Serve at room temperature on bread slices, as sandwich spread, relish, tapas etc.

Cheesy Artichoke Fondue

Yields 2 cups

2 cups	cooked artichoke hearts
1 cup	fresh basil
2	garlic cloves
Juice of 1	lemon
¼ teaspoon	lemon zest
½ cup	vegan mayonnaise dressing
1 cup	grated veggie parmesan
1½ cups	veggie mozzarella shreds
	salt and pepper

In blender, process the chokes, basil, and garlic. Mix in the remaining ingredients and season to taste. Heat until the "cheese" is melted and slightly bubbly.

Idea: Carve out a sourdough round and stuff with fondue; heat in a 350°F oven until warm and bubbly and serve with bread cubes on tooth picks. To die for!

Citrus Cavoli

Serves 12

6	mandarin oranges, peeled and sectioned
4 tablespoons	olive oil
1 medium-large	cauliflower (1 pound), cut into 1-inch pieces and parboiled
1 cup	thinly sliced scallions, including greens (about two bunches)
4	garlic cloves, thinly sliced
¾ teaspoon	sea salt
5 tablespoons	pine nuts
3 tablespoons	chopped fresh parsley
1 teaspoon	grated lemon peel
½ teaspoon	red pepper
1½ cups	diced fresh tomatoes (4-6 medium)
¼ teaspoon	saffron powder
3 tablespoons	balsamic vinegar
1 tablespoon	maple syrup
½ teaspoon	cocoa powder
½ cup	vegetable broth*

Score the orange slices once to allow the juices to escape; place in bowl. Pour 2 tablespoons of olive oil into a skillet and heat for 2 minutes. Add the cauliflower and scallions and cook for another 2 minutes. Now add the garlic, cook for 2 minutes then mix in the salt. Set aside.

Wipe the skillet clean and add the remaining oil, the pine nuts, parsley, lemon peel, and red pepper. Cook for 3 minutes then add the cauliflower mixture. Cook for 3 minutes on medium-high heat. Add the tomatoes and cook for 2 minutes more. Now add the saffron, balsamic vinegar, syrup, cocoa powder, orange slices, and vegetable broth or remaining juice (see note) and bring to a boil. Reduce the heat and simmer until the sauce is almost absorbed, 5–8 minutes. Serve warm on Italian bread slices.

If using canned orange slices, the juice in the can may be used in place of vegetable broth.

'Crab' Boats

Serves 8

1 pound	shredded veggie crab
¼ cup	diced celery
4 tablespoons	capers
1 tablespoon	powdered vegetable seasoning
¼ teaspoon	black pepper
1 teaspoon	chopped fresh mint
2 teaspoons	chopped fresh dill weed
½ teaspoon	sea salt
¾ cup	vegan mayonnaise dressing
1	head each white and red endive

Mix all the ingredients, except the endive, and refrigerate for 1 hour. Wash and separate the endive leaves and spoon the "crab" mixture onto the leaves. Place on a serving tray.

Dynamite Dolmas

Serves 6

12	grape leaves
6 tablespoons	olive oil
3 teaspoons	dry sherry
1 cup	cooked brown rice
3 teaspoons	chopped fresh parsley
¼ cup	vegan soy hamburger
1 teaspoon	cumin
¼ teaspoon	sea salt
¼ teaspoon	red pepper

Steam the grape leaves then spread them out on an oiled (use 3 tablespoons) surface to cool. Brush with the sherry.

In a skillet, place the remaining oil, the rice, parsley, "hamburger," cumin, salt, and red pepper. Brown the mixture over a medium heat for 4 minutes. Cool. Divide the mixture between the grape leaves, placing it in the center, and roll up.

Serve warm or cold. Cucumber Dressing (page 302) is a fine complement to this dish.

Eggplant Medallions

Serves 12

1	Japanese eggplant, sliced into 12
	sea salt
6	veggie mozzarella slices, cut into triangles
2	medium tomatoes, sliced into 12
	cracked pepper
12	fresh basil leaves
	olive oil

Sprinkle the eggplant slices with sea salt, place in a colander with a weight on top and drain for 1 hour. In a skillet, grill the eggplant, without any oil, for 2 minutes each side. Place the cheese triangles on top followed by the tomato slices. Sprinkle with pepper and add a basil leaf. Drizzle with oil. Place under the broiler for 2 minutes, or until the "cheese" begins to melt.

'Egg' Salad Rollups

Serves 12

1 bunch	collard greens, washed and leaves separated
2 pounds	soft tofu, rinsed
1 bunch	scallions, sliced paper thin
2	garlic cloves, minced
1 teaspoon	sea salt
1 teaspoon	white pepper
2 teaspoons	paprika
2 teaspoons	cumin
1 can	hearts of palm, each piece quartered lengthwise

Place the collard greens in boiling water and cook until tender, about 15 minutes. Remove the leaves from the water, separate them out on paper towels and pat dry.

In a blender, mix all remaining ingredients except the hearts of palm. Chill the mixture for 1 hour. Place 2–3 tablespoons of the salad on each collard leaf. Place one of the hearts of palm on top and roll up, placing the rolls end side down on a serving tray. Secure with toothpicks.

Fire and Ice

Serves 12

6	small habañero peppers, halved, seeded, and roasted
1 cup	coconut, lemon, lime, or mango sorbet

Stuff each chili half with the sorbet and freeze well.

Call 911!

Fisherman's Net

Serves 12

1 cup	hickory syrup
1 cup	virgin olive oil
12	peppercorns
12	juniper berries
½ teaspoon	creole spice
12	veggie scallops
12	veggie shrimp
6 pieces	sea vegetable
4 cups	roma tomatoes, diced with skins left on
½ cup	balsamic vinegar
2 teaspoons	ground cinnamon
¼ cup	virgin olive oil

Combine the syrup, oil, peppercorns, juniper berries, and spice. Place the "scallops" and "shrimps" in this mixture and marinate overnight.

Soak the sea vegetable in water until soft then pat dry. Cut each piece in half lengthwise. Combine the tomatoes with vinegar, oil, and cinnamon. Spread out in an ovenproof dish and bake under the broiler until bubbly and just charred. Do the same with the "seafood."

To assemble: Place the tomatoes in timbales and place on plates. Wrap the sea vegetable around the timbales for garnish. Arrange one scallop and one shrimp alongside and drizzle with hickory syrup. Serve warm.

Freshwater (Up Stream) Quesadillas

Serves 8

1	veggie salmon, diced (2 cups)
2 teaspoons	sea salt
2 teaspoons	pepper
1 teaspoon	cumin
1	large white onion, chopped
6	garlic cloves, chopped
12 tablespoons	vegetable margarine
3	plum tomatoes, diced
½ cup	limejuice
16	small corn tortillas
2 cups	veggie mozzarella, shredded
6 teaspoons	powdered vegetable seasoning
3 teaspoons	fresh purple basil, chopped
3	limes, wedged

Preheat the oven to 350°F.

In a skillet, flash cook the salmon with the salt, pepper, cumin, onion, garlic, and 1 tablespoon of the margarine for 5 minutes. Add the tomatoes and lime juice.

Baste each tortilla with some margarine. Divide the "salmon" between 8 tortillas. Follow with the shredded veggie cheese. Top with a corn tortilla, baste with a little more margarine, and sprinkle with vegetable seasoning. Bake for 5 minutes, turning over once. Cut each tortilla into four pieces, sprinkle with the basil and serve immediately with the lime wedges. Red or Haute Mango Salsa (pages 329 and 328) are good accompaniments.

Variation:
Cook the "salmon" with 1 cup limejuice, 2 tablespoons

powdered vegetable seasoning, 1 tablespoon dill, 2 cloves minced garlic, 1 teaspoon pepper, and 3 cups fresh spinach ... and use veggie cheddar instead of mozzarella.

Fond of Fondue... Cape Aire Cheddar

Serves 8 or more

½ pound	vegan soy hamburger
6 tablespoons	vegetable margarine
1	yellow onion, chopped
1	garlic clove
6 tablespoons	flour
2 cups	soymilk
16 ounces	veggie cheddar cheese, shredded
1 cup	organic beer
4 ounces	green chilies
Pinch of	sea salt
½ teaspoon	black pepper
	baguette rounds, cubed
	pear slices

Cook the veggie hamburger in 3 tablespoons of margarine, breaking it up as it cooks. Remove from the pan, add the remaining margarine and sauté the onion and garlic in it.

Add the flour, stirring constantly to form a roux. Add the soymilk and stir until thickened. Return the "hamburger" crumbles to the pan and add the veggie cheddar and organic beer. Continue stirring until melted. Add the chilies and season with salt and pepper. Use the bread and pears for dipping. Great for Super Bowl.

Got Hot Wings?

Serves 6

2 cups	veggie chicken, cubed
1 cup	hickory syrup
5 tablespoons	bottled chili sauce
1	yellow onion, diced
3 tablespoons	cider vinegar
1 tablespoon	Dijon mustard
1 teaspoon	vegan Worcestershire sauce
6	wooden skewers

Place the "chicken" in a shallow dish. Combine the remaining ingredients and pour over the "chicken." Leave to marinate for 6 hours, turning every so often. Skewer the "chicken" and bake in a 350°F oven, or barbecue it, until lightly browned.

Greek Toasts

Serves 8 or more

2 cups	soy cream cheese
½ cup	kalamata olives
½ cup	sun-dried tomatoes, snipped into small pieces
1	small cucumber, peeled
2 teaspoons	capers, well rinsed
8 slices	favorite bread, trimmed of crusts and sliced into triangles
2 teaspoons	black pepper
4 tablespoons	lemon juice
4 tablespoons	olive oil
2 teaspoon	chopped fresh parsley
	onion powder

In food processor combine the cream cheese, olives, tomatoes, cucumber, and capers.

Spread the filling on one toast triangle and top with another. Mix the pepper, lemon juice, oil, and parsley together. Dip each "sandwich" in the mixture and place in a 375°F oven until browned and filling is bubbly. Garnish with onion powder.

Serve warm.

Grilled Cheese Shish Kabob

Serves 4–6

8 ounces	tofu cheddar cheese block, cut into cubes
1 loaf	French bread, cut into cubes
6 ounces	sun-dried tomatoes
½ cup	olive oil
3	garlic cloves, minced
3 teaspoons	sea salt
	barbecue

Light the barbecue and heat the coals.

Place the "cheese" cubes, bread, and tomatoes on skewers. Mix the oil, garlic and salt. Baste the skewered foodstuffs with the mixture. Grill on the barbecue for 5 minutes or until bread is crisp and cheese begins to soften

Key Lime Avocado Rapture

Serves 4

1 cup	raw sugar
6	key limes, juiced (grate 2½ teaspoons peel or zest from the limes and set aside)
1 cup	corn syrup
4	large avocados, peeled, sliced, and chopped
3 tablespoons	minced fresh cilantro
1 cup	chopped tomatoes
1	jalapeño pepper
	a few cilantro leaves

Place the sugar in a saucepan with 1 cup of water and bring to a boil, stirring until the sugar dissolves. Set aside to cool. Place the limejuice in a saucepan with 1 cup of water and boil. Add the sugar syrup and corn syrup. Refrigerate until cold. Pour the chilled sorbet base into an ice cream maker and process according to manufacturer's instructions. Combine the avocado, cilantro, and 2 teaspoons of the lime zest. Divide the mixture into four portions and place in a "stack-up" or timbales.

Scoop out the sorbet and pack it into the timbales on top of the avocado. Refrigerate for 1–2 hours.

Meanwhile, purée the tomatoes and pepper and set aside. To serve, turn over and plate each timbale. Drizzle the tomatoes over the stack and garnish with cilantro and lime zest.

Lobster Wonton Appetizer

Serves 12

1	veggie lobster, finely diced
1 cup	finely diced celery
3	garlic cloves, minced
1 cup	finely diced baby portobellos
3 tablespoons	hickory syrup
Juice of 2	limes
¼ cup	chopped chives
4-6 dashes	hot sauce
1 tablespoon	truffle oil
Juice of 1	lime
	salt and pepper to taste
1 package	wonton wrappers (or spring rolls for larger appetites!)
	flour wash (1 teaspoon flour with 1 tablespoon water)
1 cup	chopped romaine or shaved fennel

Combine all ingredients except the wonton skins, flour wash, and romaine/fennel.

Spoon the filling into each skin and brush the edges with the flour wash. Fold in half into triangles then fold the two corners back again.

Fry the wontons in hot vegetable oil (350°F) until golden brown. Drain on paper towels. Serve over a bed of romaine tossed in limejuice. Pineapple Papaya or Haute Mango Salsa (pages 329 and 328 are good accompaniments).

Mediterranean Tapas

Serves 8

8 slices	**veggie bacon**
16	**roasted almonds**
16	**green olives**
16	**pitted dates**
16	**toothpicks**

Cook the "bacon" according to instructions, but slice each piece in half prior to cooking.

Place an almond inside each olive. Place an olive inside each date.

Wrap the "bacon" slices around the dates. Secure with toothpicks and serve.

Mexi Cali Crostini

Yields 30 plus

½ cup	black beans, soaked overnight and drained
3	garlic cloves, minced
1	bay leaf
2 tablespoons	cumin
3 tablespoons	olive oil
1 teaspoon	limejuice
	salt and pepper
½	green bell pepper, finely diced
1	mango, finely diced
1	large French baguette, cut into ½-inch thick slices and toasted
6 ounces	pickled jalapeño pepper slices

Put the beans in a large kettle and cover them with water. Add the garlic and bay leaf and simmer until tender, about 1½ hours. Remove from heat, drain water and discard the bay leaf. Add the cumin, oil, and limejuice. Process until smooth and season with salt and pepper. Fold in the bell pepper and mango. Allow flavors to meld for 1 hour or more.

To assemble the crostini, spread the beans on slices of baguette and top with a pickled pepper.

Miso Caraway Spread on Melba Toasts

Serves 12

3 ounces	soy cream cheese
5 tablespoons	white miso
3 tablespoons	chopped shallot
1 teaspoon	caraway seeds
½ teaspoon	black pepper
¼ cup	chopped chives
10 ounces	almond cheddar cheese, cut into ½-inch pieces
¼ cup	vegetable margarine, melted
12	melba toasts

Puree all the ingredients except the almond cheddar, margarine, and melba toast. Add the bite-sized almond cheddar to the mixture last and blend lightly to leave some chunks.

Dip the toasts in the melted margarine and place in oven for about 3 minutes at 425°F.

Place a tablespoon of dip on each toast and serve.

Mushroom Marsala

Serves 8

3 teaspoons	olive oil
2	large shallots, finely diced
6	garlic cloves, finely chopped
½ teaspoon	black pepper
2 pounds	small brown mushrooms
2 cups	organic Marsala
1	baguette, sliced into 1-inch thick slices

In a skillet, heat the olive oil. Add the shallot, garlic, and pepper and sauté gently for a few minutes. Add the mushrooms and continue to sauté for 4 minutes. Add the Marsala and gently simmer until wine is reduced to ½ cup and the mushrooms are plump. Serve with the baguette slices.

Nilonese Dim Sum

Yields 12 buns

Dough:
2 tablespoons	cane sugar
1 cup	warm water
1 tablespoon	active yeast
3 cups	all-purpose flour
1 tablespoon	vegetable margarine
1 teaspoon	baking powder

Stuffing:
1 cup	veggie pork
1	scallion, chopped
2 tablespoons	tamari
2 tablespoons	water
½ teaspoon	pepper
½ teaspoon	cornstarch

For the dough: Dissolve the sugar in the water, add the yeast and allow to sit at room temperature until the yeast begins to foam up, about 10 minutes. Add the yeast mixture to the flour and combine, mixing well. Add the margarine and baking powder. Turn out on to a floured surface and knead into a dough. Knead for 5 minutes then turn back into a bowl and cover with a cloth. Allow to rise for about 2 hours until it has doubled in volume. Roll out on a floured surface again and form into a long rolling pin shape. Cut into 12 pieces then roll into balls. Place the balls on parchment paper and cover again for 30 minutes.

For the stuffing: Mix the "pork" with the onion, tamari, water, and pepper in a saucepan. Heat then add the cornstarch and heat for a few minutes to thicken it.

Divide each ball of dough in half, make a small indentation in one half and place some filling inside. Cover up the filling with the other piece of dough and roll into a ball, completely encapsulating the filling. Place the balls in a bamboo steamer and cook over boiling water for 12 minutes.

Serve warm or cold.

Nuccio's Rollatini

Serves 6

4-ounce jar	roasted red peppers
1	garlic clove, minced
¼ cup	chopped fresh parsley
1 tablespoon	olive oil
1 teaspoon	balsamic vinegar
Pinch of	salt
6 slices	veggie ham
12 slices	veggie provolone
12 slices	veggie salami
12 slices	veggie Swiss soy cheese
	toothpicks

Combine the first six ingredients and set aside for 20 minutes to allow the flavors to mix.

Layer the veggie ham, provolone, salami, and Swiss "cheese" down the middle of a long piece of plastic wrap or foil. Spoon the pepper mixture down the middle and roll tightly like a cigar. Wrap tightly in the plastic wrap or foil and refrigerate overnight. Remove wrap, place toothpicks through the cigar, cut and serve.

'Over the Top!' Artichoke Bruschetta

Serves 8

2 cups	baby artichoke hearts
1 teaspoon	chopped fresh thyme
3 teaspoons	chopped fresh parsley
4 tablespoons	olive oil
2	garlic cloves, minced
1	lemon, juiced and zest retained
½ cup	veggie caraway cheese
1 loaf	sourdough bread, sliced thick
1 bunch	arugula, washed and patted dry
	balsamic vinegar

In a skillet, cook the chokes and herbs in olive oil until slightly crispy, adding the garlic when the chokes are almost cooked. Drain and pat dry. Take 1 cup of the chokes and process, adding the lemon juice and "cheese". Set the remaining chokes aside. Sprinkle olive oil over the sourdough slices and put under oven broiler for 2 minutes, or until lightly toasted.

To assemble: Divide the arugula between the sourdough slices, place a heaping spoonful of choke spread on top, sprinkle some lemon zest over and finish with a spoonful of retained chokes.

Broil again for 1 minute or so then drizzle with balsamic vinegar.

Pizzazz! Fondue

Serves 6

1 pound	vegan soy hamburger
1	yellow onion, chopped
3	garlic cloves, minced
12	ripe tomatoes, diced
1 can (3oz)	tomato paste
1 teaspoon	each fresh basil, oregano, and sage
1½ cups	veggie provolone shreds
1½ cups	veggie mozzarella shreds
1 loaf	French bread, cubed

Sauté the soy hamburger crumbles, onion, and garlic. Add the rest of ingredients (except the bread) and heat until the "cheeses" are melting and bubbly. Dip in the bread cubes. Pizza On A Stick!

Quesadillas Supreme ... Olé!

Serves 6–12

1 cup	fresh pole beans, cleaned and cut into 2-inch pieces
3	large portobello mushrooms, sliced
¼	large white onion, thinly sliced
1	garlic clove, minced
2 teaspoons	pepper
3 teaspoons	vegan taco seasoning
½ cup	organic beer
6	large flour tortillas
8 tablespoons	olive oil
1½ cups	shredded veggie cheddar cheese
¼ cup	grated veggie parmesan
	veggie sour cream
	Red Salsa (page 329)
	Guacamole "Dressing" (page 303)

Preheat the oven to 350°F.

In a skillet, sauté the beans, mushrooms, onion, garlic, pepper, and taco seasoning in 2 tablespoons of the oil for 6 minutes. Deglaze with organic beer and simmer 6 minutes more.

Baste 3 tortillas with olive oil. Sprinkle with half the veggie cheddar. Spoon the vegetable mixture over the shredded cheese and top with tortilla. Baste again and add more veggie cheddar followed by grated Parmesan. Top with a tortilla, baste with oil again and sprinkle with taco seasoning. Bake for 7 minutes. Cut each tortilla into six pieces and serve immediately.

Serve with sour cream, Red Salsa, and Guacamole "Dressing".

Quinoa Poblanos

Serves 8

1½ cups	vegetable broth
¾ cup	quinoa
2 teaspoons	olive oil
1 cup	chopped mixed red, green, yellow bell pepper
½ cup	chopped onion
1	jalapeño pepper, minced
2	garlic cloves, minced
2 tablespoons	pumpkin seeds
½ cup	sliced scallions
1 tablespoon	chopped fresh cilantro
1 tablespoon	tamari
4	poblano chilis, cleaned, seeded, and cut in half
1 tablespoon	limejuice
2 cups	mild salsa or Red Salsa (page 329)
1 cup	veggie mozzarella, shredded

Preheat the oven to 350°F.

In a saucepan bring the broth and quinoa to a boil, reduce heat, cover, and simmer for 15 minutes. In a skillet, heat the oil and sauté the bell peppers, onion, jalapeño, and garlic for 2 minutes. Add the pumpkin seeds and scallions and continue to sauté for 2 minutes more. Remove from the heat.

Stir in the quinoa, cilantro, tamari, and limejuice. Spoon ⅓ cup of the mixture into each chili.

Pour the salsa into an ovenproof baking dish (13 x 9 inch). Place each chili half in the dish and bake for 20 minutes. Sprinkle with the cheese and bake for another 10 minutes.

Scrumptious Samosas

Yields 10

Pastry:

2 cups	wheat or barley flour
½ cup	white vinegar
¼ cup	safflower oil
1 teaspoon	salt
	water

Filling:

2 teaspoons	coriander
¼ teaspoon	red pepper
¼ teaspoon	ginger
1 tablespoon	garam masala
1 teaspoon	cumin
1 teaspoon	safflower oil
1	garlic clove, minced
2	scallions, diced
2 cups	diced veggies i.e. potatoes, cauliflower, okra, tomato, spinach, etc.
3 tablespoons	lemon juice

Combine the pastry ingredients and add enough water to form a dough. Divide the dough into 5 equal balls. Roll each ball into a 7-inch circle. Stack all the dough circles on top of each other. Heat a teflon skillet and place the dough stack in the center, allowing it to warm up for 1 minute or so. Peel each layer off and restack. Cut each circle in half.

Place the seasonings in a heated skillet with the safflower oil. Heat for about 1 minute then add the garlic, scallions, and veggies. Cook for 3 minutes then add lemon juice. Remove from the heat and cool.

Roll each half circle of dough into a cone, overlapping the edges, and dampen and pinch to seal. Stuff the cones with the filling and then pinch the open end closed to form a triangle. Bake in a 350°F oven until browned and crisp, about 13–15 minutes.

Serve with your favorite chutney.

'Seafood' Timbale in Wasabi Sauce

Serves 8

½ quantity	Tempeh "No Tuna" Salad recipe (page 83)
¼ quantity	Sushi Rice recipe (page 168)
Full quantity	Not Salmon Pate! recipe (page 342)
Full quantity	Wasabi Sauce recipe (page 219)
8	veggie shrimp
4 tablespoons	lemon juice
2 teaspoons	green tea
4 pieces	seaweed or sea vegetable, soaked in water and cut into thin strips
8 tablespoons	sesame seeds, toasted
1 cup	sprouts (your favorite)
	sesame oil

Oil 8 small timbales. Pack the tempeh salad on the bottom of each, followed by the sushi rice. Pack in the "salmon" pate. Refrigerate for 1 hour. Marinate the "shrimp" in the lemon juice and green tea.

To assemble: Spoon the wasabi sauce onto the serving plates. Unmold the timbales onto the plates and place thin strips of seaweed around the timbales. Sprinkle the toasted sesame seeds over the timbales and garnish the tops with one shrimp and the sprouts.

Spring Rolls

Serves 12

4 tablespoons	safflower oil
1 tablespoon	grated ginger root
1 teaspoon	white pepper
3 tablespoons	tamari
3 tablespoons	chopped fresh parsley
12	large wonton wrappers
½ cup	water chestnuts, diced
1 cup	shredded bok choy
½ cup	mushrooms, chopped
2	carrots, grated
5	veggie shrimp, diced and chopped
4 tablespoons	lemon juice
4 tablespoons	soft tofu

Heat the oil in a skillet. Flash-cook the ginger and pepper
with the tamari and parsley. Add the vegetables; stir-fry for
4 minutes then toss with the lemon juice.

Lay out the wrappers and divide the vegetable mixture
between them, placing it in the middle of the wrappers. Process
the tofu with 2 tablespoons of water, brush this on the edges
of the wontons. Fold and press to seal. Fry until golden brown,
about 3 minutes.

Serve with sweet 'n' sour, plum sauce, etc.

Strawberry Nachos

Serves 12

12	4-inch corn tortillas
2 teaspoons	olive oil
2 teaspoons	cumin
¼ cup	minced celery
Juice of 1	lime
	salt and pepper
1 cup	Guacamole "Dressing" (page 303)
1 cup	Strawberry Salsa (page 330)
½ cup	veggie sour cream
	some fresh cilantro

Lay out the corn tortillas. Brush with oil and sprinkle with cumin, celery, limejuice, and salt and pepper. Cut into quarters. Bake in a 350°F oven for 4 minutes.

Spoon the guacamole over the tortilla chips, then follow with the salsa. Top with another chip and a dollop of sour cream. Garnish with cilantro and serve immediately.

Stuffed Portobello Mushrooms

Serves 6

3 tablespoons	olive oil
¾ pound	vegan soy hamburger
¼ cup	thinly sliced scallions (including greens)
1	garlic clove, minced
6	medium portobello mushrooms, stems removed and diced
½ teaspoon	sea salt
½ teaspoon	white pepper
¼ teaspoon	each of oregano, basil, thyme, rosemary (preferably fresh)
¼ cup	finely diced celery, parboiled
½ cup	organic beer
½ cup	tomato juice
1 cup	bread crumbs
3 tablespoons	vegetable margarine, melted

Preheat the oven to 375°F. Line a cookie sheet with aluminum foil.

Heat 2 tablespoons of the olive oil in a skillet. Add the burger, scallions, garlic, mushroom stems, salt, and pepper and cook until the crumbles are browned. Remove the mixture from the heat and set aside.

Wipe the skillet, add the remaining 1 tablespoon of olive oil and heat. Add the herbs and celery; sear together then remove from the heat. Combine the burger mixture and herbs in mixing bowl. Add the organic beer, tomato juice, and bread crumbs. The mixture should stick together. Fill the mushrooms with the mixture (approximately 2–3 tablespoons each cap).

Brush the cookie sheet with some of the melted margarine, place the mushroom caps on the sheet and brush the tops with the remaining margarine. Cover with aluminum foil and cook in the oven for 15–20 minutes. Uncover the mushrooms and place under the broiler for 5 minutes to brown.

Squash Blossom Special

Serves 12

12	squash blossoms
6	scallions, minced (reserve green tops)
½ cup	roasted peanuts, chopped
2 cups	soy cream cheese
½ cup	chopped bell pepper
½ cup	veggie parmesan
2 tablespoons	chopped fresh parsley and chives
	salt and pepper
1 cup	flour
1 cup	organic beer
	red pepper

Set the squash blossoms aside and mix all the remaining ingredients, except the flour and beer, in a bowl. Stuff the blossoms with the mixture and tie them securely with the green scallion tops.

Combine the flour and organic beer and season with red pepper. Adjust batter as desired (more or less beer), then dip each blossom in the batter and fry in safflower oil for 30 seconds. Drain on a rack before serving.

'Tater' Skins

Serves 6

3	medium russet potatoes, halved
1 tablespoon	powdered vegetable seasoning
½ cup	multigrain milk
2 tablespoons	olive oil
¼ cup	minced red tomatoes
¼ cup	minced yellow onions
¼ cup	minced bell peppers
1	garlic clove, minced
6 ounces	shredded veggie cheese, any flavor
3 tablespoons	vegetable margarine

Rinse the potatoes in water and bake in the oven at 450°F oven for 20 minutes.

Remove the potato flesh from the skins and place in a saucepan. Place the potato skins on an aluminum foil-covered cookie sheet, sprinkle over the vegetable seasoning and milk and return them to the oven to bake for another 6 minutes.

Add the oil, tomato, onion, bell pepper, and garlic to the saucepan containing the potato flesh. Cook for 3 minutes. Spoon the mixture into the potato skins. Top with cheese and margarine and bake for 6–8 minutes.

'Tea-Time' Sandwiches

Serves 6

6 slices	pumpernickel bread, crusts removed
3 tablespoons	crunchy peanut butter
3 tablespoons	sweet pickle relish
3 tablespoons	veggie sour cream or veggie cottage cheese

Spread 1 tablespoon of peanut butter, sour cream, and pickle relish on three of the bread slices. Cover them with them with the remaining bread slices and cut, criss-cross, into triangles.

Teriyaki "Chicken" Nuggets

Serves 4

1 teaspoon	olive oil
¼ cup	chopped white onion
1 cup	tamari
½ cup	pineapple juice
3	garlic cloves, minced
1 tablespoon	maple syrup
½ teaspoon	grated ginger root
¼ teaspoon	red-pepper flakes
1 package	veggie "chicken" nuggets

Heat the olive oil in small skillet, add the onion, and cook for 2 minutes. Mix in the rest of the ingredients, except the nuggets, and remove from the heat. Place the veggie nuggets in a dish and add the sauce. Cover and refrigerate overnight.

Preheat the broiler to 475°F. Place the nuggets on skewers, brush with the sauce and broil. Turn and brush the nuggets frequently. Broil until sauce and nuggets appear glazed and brown, about 10–12 minutes.

Thai-Style Spicy Spring Rolls

Serves 4–8

1 tablespoon	vegan mayonnaise dressing
1 tablespoon	roasted sesame seed (black)
Juice of 1	lime
1 cup	veggie shrimp or lobster, diced
4–8	spring roll wrappers (or rice paper)
1 cup	exotic-mix salad greens
1	cucumber, julienne cut
1	carrot, julienne cut
1	mango, julienne cut
1	papaya, julienne cut
1 bunch	cilantro, chopped
4	scallions, diced
8	mint leaves

Combine the "mayo," sesame seed, limejuice, and veggie seafood. Set aside.

Lay out the wrappers or soak the rice paper until soft and lay out. Divide the greens, julienne items, seafood mixture, cilantro, scallions, and mint between the wrappers. Fold in the ends and roll up, burrito style. Brush the ends with water and seal.

These are delicious served with peanut sauce (mix 2 tablespoons peanut butter and 1 cup coconut milk) and Thai Chili Sauce (from a specialty store). Slice in half and garnish with spring flowers (choose rose, hibiscus, squash blossom), additional exotic greens and enoki mushroom.

TJ Landing's "Chinese Dumpling Party"

Serves 24

2 blocks	firm tofu
	safflower oil
	wonton wrappers
	dipping sauce
1 cup	thinly sliced mushrooms
½ cup	thinly sliced scallions
3 tablespoons	walnuts, minced
1	garlic clove, minced
3 tablespoons	chopped fresh parsley
1	winter squash, roasted
1	red bell pepper, roasted
½ cup	thinly sliced scallions
1 teaspoon	ginger
1 bunch	spinach, chopped
1 teaspoon	chopped fresh dill
2 tablespoons	chopped fresh parsley
1 teaspoon	chopped fresh basil
3 tablespoons	pine nuts, toasted
2	sweet potatoes, roasted
1 cup	black beans
1	jalapeño chili, roasted
2	garlic cloves, minced
½ teaspoon	cinnamon
Pinch of	nutmeg

Set aside the first four ingredients on the list and combine each of the remaining groupings of ingredients in large mixing bowls. Cut the firm tofu blocks in half. Puree each tofu block with the contents of each mixing bowl, respectively. Party members may fold their own combinations. Fry the wontons until they pop, about 1 minute, then steam them over vegetable broth for 2 minutes or so.

Serve with a sauce: a mixture of 1 cup tamari, 1 cup rice wine vinegar, ½ teaspoon sesame seed, and 2 minced scallions is good.

Vegetable Bouquet

Serves 24

1	very large head cabbage
12	cherry tomatoes
12	white mushrooms
12	broccoli florets
12	cauliflower florets
12	jicama cubes
12	fluted carrot slices
12	fluted scallions
12	fluted celery sticks
12	radish "flowers"
6	yellow bell pepper slices
6	red bell pepper slices
6	orange bell pepper slices
6	green bell pepper slices
12	asparagus spears, steamed then chilled
12	very small Brussels sprouts, steamed then chilled
6	very small red potatoes, parboiled 8 minutes and chilled
3	small salad cucumbers, cut into three pieces
12	bread sticks
Plenty of	wooden skewers
1	large basket

Prepare the vegetables as directed in the ingredients list Line the basket with the appropriate choice of table linen and place the cabbage in the center. Place the vegetables on skewers and pierce into the cabbage, arranging the vegetables in a bouquet. Serve with the bread sticks and your favorite dips, sauces, or fondue.

Veggie In-a-Blanket

Serves 12

8	veggie dogs, each piece cut into 3
1 quantity	Quick-Rise Bread Dough recipe (see page 385)
½ cup	vegetable margarine, melted
½ cup	pecans, finely chopped
6 tablespoons	maple syrup

Preheat the oven to 400°F.

Roll out the dough to the shape of a large pizza and cut into 24 triangles. Place a piece of veggie dog on the long end of a triangle and roll up. Repeat with the remaining triangles.

Combine the rest of the ingredients in a shallow baking dish. Roll each blanket in the mixture and line up, seam down, in the dish. Bake for 15 minutes or until brown.

Veggie Taquitos

Serves 8

8	**small corn tortillas**
1 package	**veggie baloney or 1 package veggie turkey slices**
2	**limes**
	safflower oil
	Guacamole "Dressing" (page 303)

Lay out the tortillas. Divide the veggie meat between the tortillas. Sprinkle limejuice over the tortillas and roll. *

Heat a skillet and add oil for frying. Fry the taquitos and serve immediately with the Guacamole.

*For variety, substitute 1½ cups Smashed Potatoes (page 216) for the veggie meat and mix in 3 tablespoons Red Salsa (page 329), roll and fry.

Waldorf Canapés

Serves 12

Base:
2	granny smith apples, peeled, cored, and sliced into rounds
2 teaspoons	lemon juice
1	small baguette, sliced into thin rounds
1	garlic clove, minced
2 teaspoons	olive oil

Filling:
1 cup	veggie cheddar, shredded
1 cup	soy cream cheese
½ cup	chopped walnuts

Garnish:
½ cup	thinly sliced onions
½ cup	rice vinegar
1	apple, shredded
	grape halves

First prepare the bases. Dip the apple rounds in the lemon juice and set aside. Combine the garlic and olive oil, spread on the bread slices and toast in the oven until lightly browned.

Combine the "filling" ingredients in a food processor.

Place the onions in a skillet with the vinegar; sauté. Add the apple and cook very briefly. Cool.

To assemble the canapés, place the filling on the apple slices and baguette rounds. Top with the garnish and grapes.

Where's The "Beef"?
Burgundy Fondue

Serves 6

16 ounces	veggie beef
3	garlic cloves, minced
1 pound	white mushrooms
2 tablespoons	minced white onion
1 teaspoon	fresh thyme
1 tablespoon	chopped fresh parsley
1	bay leaf
3 tablespoons	extra virgin olive oil
1 teaspoon	black pepper
⅓ cup	rye flour
1½ cups	red wine
1 teaspoon	salt
20	pearl onions

Combine the veggie beef, garlic, mushroom, minced onion, and herbs. Marinate overnight.

Heat the olive oil in a saucepan and add the "beef" mixture; sauté. Remove the "beef" and sprinkle with flour; place marinade in processor and blend. Place the processed marinade in a fondue pot, add the onions, and heat. Add the wine and heat until the onions are tender. Add the "beef" just before serving – guests may skewer the "beef" fondue.

Wow! Luau Fondue

Serves 4 plus

2 cups	veggie pork
1 cup	sliced pineapple
¼ cup	pineapple juice
¼ cup	tamari
¼ cup	maple syrup
¼ cup	ketchup
½ teaspoon	ground mace
	sea salt
	banana leaves and hibiscus flower to garnish
	wooden skewers

Set aside the veggie pork and sliced pineapple and heat together all the remaining ingredients. Adjust salt to taste and simmer for 30 minutes.

Place the banana leaves on a platter, arrange the pineapple and veggie pork on top and garnish with a hibiscus flower.

Serve the fondue sauce with the platter, and the skewers so guests can help themselves.

Salads:

GREENS, FRUITS, GRAINS,

AND MARINATED VEGETABLES

Salads are refreshingly cool on warm
days and easy to prepare—as an
introduction to the entrée, with a
bowl of soup, or by themselves.
Fresh! Fresh!

Blood Orange with Belgium Endive in Hickory Shagbark Vinaigrette

Serves 2

2 teaspoons	sliced almonds
¼ cup	hickory shagbark syrup
¼ cup	balsamic vinegar
Juice of 1	honey tangerine
2	Belgium endive, rinsed and leaves separated
2	blood oranges, sliced

Place the almonds on a cookie sheet and toast at 375°F until golden brown.

Mix the syrup, vinegar, and tangerine juice in bottle, shaking well.

Arrange the endive and oranges on a plate. Drizzle with the vinaigrette and sprinkle with almonds.

Stuffed Chokes

Serves 4–8

4	large artichokes, trimmed and chokes removed
1 quantity	Tempeh "No Tuna" Salad recipe (see page 83)
4 teaspoons	vegetable margarine
1 cup	bread crumbs
¼ cup	extra virgin olive oil
¼ cup	balsamic vinegar
1 teaspoon	fresh oregano
	salt and pepper

Steam the artichokes then spoon out the centers and discard. Fill the hollowed out shells with the tempeh salad.

Mix the margarine with the bread crumbs and top up the chokes with the mixture. Mix the oil, vinegar, and oregano; season with salt and pepper. Drizzle with the vinaigrette and put the chokes under the broiler to brown the tops. Once set you can cut the chokes in half or you can serve them whole.

Chopstick Salad

Serves 4

1 head	romaine lettuce, chopped
1 cup	red chard, chopped
2 cups	oyster mushrooms
1 cup	bean sprouts
1 cup	snow peas
	Sesame Dressing (page 306)

Wash all the vegetables well. Toss them together in a large bowl and serve with the Sesame Dressing.

Curried Tempeh Salad

Serves 8

1 cup	tempeh
2 teaspoons	tamari
3 tablespoons	curry powder
¼ cup	very finely chopped red onion
¼ cup	sliced almonds
½ cup	favorite chutney
1 cup	green seedless grapes, halved
½ cup	cooked wild or brown rice
¼ cup	very finely chopped celery
½ cup	vegan mayonnaise dressing
	salt and pepper to taste
2 cups	shredded radicchio
2 cups	shredded iceberg lettuce
1 cup	baby spinach
¼ cup	"Taste of Honey" Dressing (page 307)

Crumble the tempeh and cook in the tamari with the curry powder, onion, and almonds until brown. Cool completely.

Mix in the rest of the ingredients, except the lettuces and dressing, and chill.

Toss the iceberg and radicchio with the spinach; mix with the dressing and allow to stand at room temperature 7 minutes until wilted. Serve the tempeh over the lettuce.

Fingerling Asparagus in Raspberry Vinaigrette

Serves 4

1 bunch	fresh asparagus, steamed until tender
½ cup	kalamata olives, pitted
½ cup	pickled red peppers

Raspberry Vinaigrette:

1 cup	red wine vinegar
½ cup	safflower oil
1 tablespoon	raw sugar
	pinch of salt
1 clove	garlic, minced
1 tablespoon	minced onion
1 teaspoon	fresh thyme
1 basket	raspberries, washed well

Mix all the vinaigrette ingredients in blender.

Gently mix the asparagus, olives, and peppers together and pour the vinaigrette over the salad. Serve warm or at room temperature.

Hal's Marinated Vegetables

Serves 6

½ pound	baby carrots, washed and parboiled
1	medium red onion, thinly sliced
½ pound	white mushrooms, washed and halved
½ pound	green beans, washed, cut up and parboiled
½	green bell pepper, washed and chopped
½ head	cauliflower, washed, cut into 1-inch pieces and parboiled

Marinade:

½ cup	wine vinegar
½ cup	olive oil
¾ cup	pineapple juice
2 teaspoons	chopped fresh thyme
2 teaspoons	chopped fresh marjoram
½ teaspoon	red-pepper flakes
1 teaspoon	powdered vegetable seasoning
2 teaspoons	maple syrup

Place all the vegetables in a bowl. Combine the marinade ingredients in a jar, shake well, and pour over the vegetables. Marinate in the refrigerator 48–72 hours, stirring twice a day.

Hearts of Palm Salad

Serves 4–6

Salad:

1 head	romaine lettuce, each leaf torn into three pieces
4	vine-ripened tomatoes, coarsely chopped
1 can	hearts of palm, each vegetable sliced into ½-inch sections
½ handful	fresh parsley, chopped

Dressing:

½ cup	tangerine orange juice
¼ cup	balsamic vinegar
¼ cup	olive oil
3 tablespoons	chopped fresh tarragon

Place the salad ingredients in a large bowl. Place the dressing ingredients in a bottle and shake well. Pour the dressing over the salad and toss well. Bring to room temperature and allow the lettuce to wilt before serving.

Herbed Melon Salad
in Lime Vinaigrette

Serves 4

½ teaspoon	sesame oil
3 tablespoons	black sesame seeds
6 cups	watercress, cleaned and washed very well
4 cups	watermelon, cut into triangles
½ cup	minced shallots
½ cup	chopped fresh chervil
¼ cup	chopped fresh parsley
⅔ cup	lime vinaigrette (mix juice of 2 limes, ¼ cup rice vinegar, ¼ cup sesame oil, 2 tablespoons apple juice, dash salt and freshly ground black pepper)

Heat the sesame oil in a skillet, add the sesame seed and shallot and toast them. Cool.

Mix the rest of the ingredients with the sesame mixture and add the lime vinaigrette just before serving.

Jiffy Bean Salad

Serves 8

Dressing:

½ cup	olive oil
1 cup	white wine vinegar
3 teaspoons	powdered vegetable seasoning
1 teaspoon	each chopped fresh sage and thyme
4 teaspoons	chopped fresh parsley
¼ cup	orange juice
¼ cup	maple syrup
½ cup	northern white beans
½ cup	garbanzo beans
½ cup	kidney beans
1 cup	green beans
1 cup	wax beans
½	large onion, thinly sliced
	salt and pepper

Mix oil and vinegar with the seasoning and herbs. Add the orange juice and syrup and combine thoroughly.

Toss the beans and onion together. Pour the dressing over the vegetables and coat well. Season to taste with salt and pepper. Refrigerate overnight before serving.

German Potato Salad

Serves 12

6 ounces	tempeh bacon
1	red onion, thinly sliced
¼ cup	maple syrup
6	yukon gold potatoes, boiled and peeled, then quartered
2	celery ribs, diced
4 tablespoons	fresh dill
1 cup	water
½ cup	wheat flour
1 cup	apple cider vinegar
	salt and pepper

Place the "bacon" and onion in a skillet with the syrup and fry until the onion softens. Add the potatoes, celery, and dill. Mix the water with the flour and slowly add this to the pan, stirring often. Add the vinegar and simmer until sauce is thickened. Season to taste with salt and pepper.

Madame Pickle's Salad

Makes about 4 pints

12	salad cucumbers, sliced very thin
1 bunch	scallions, sliced thin, bottoms only
2 tablespoons	sea salt
	crushed ice
1 tablespoon	powdered vegetable seasoning
1 tablespoon	celery seed
2 cups	maple syrup
1 cup	white vinegar

Combine the cucumbers and scallions with the salt, add enough crushed ice to cover them then refrigerate overnight.

Combine the vegetable seasoning, celery seed, syrup, and vinegar in saucepan. Bring to a boil and cook for 1 minute. Remove from heat.

Rinse the cucumbers well. Pour the syrup mixture over cucumbers and refrigerate. You can also freeze the salad for later use. Serve as a side dish with tempura or sushi.

Marinated Bow Tie Pasta Salad

Serves 8

1 cup	bow tie pasta shells
½ cup	red onion rings
¾ cup	artichoke hearts, quartered
1 cup	mushrooms, quartered
¾ cup	cherry tomatoes
½ cup	black olives, sliced
½ cup	olive oil
¼ cup	red wine vinegar
1 teaspoon	capers
½ teaspoon	fresh thyme
½ teaspoon	fresh oregano
½ teaspoon	pepper
2	garlic cloves, minced
½ cup	shredded veggie parmesan

Cook the pasta according to package directions. Drain and cool. Place the veggies and pasta in a mixing bowl.

Mix the oil, vinegar, capers, herbs, pepper, and garlic. Pour the dressing over the pasta salad and marinate overnight in the refrigerator.

Sprinkle the chilled salad with the veggie parmesan just before serving.

Mushroom Confetti

Serves 6

½ pound	assorted small mushrooms, trimmed and cleaned
1	red bell pepper, julienne cut
1	white onion, thinly sliced
½ cup	olive oil
2 tablespoons	lemon juice
2	garlic cloves
2 tablespoons	finely chopped fresh parsley
½ teaspoon	cumin
	salt and pepper

Place the mushrooms, red pepper, and onion in a bowl. Whisk together the oil, lemon juice, garlic, parsley, and cumin. Pour the dressing over the vegetables and season with salt and pepper. Marinate for 1 hour and serve at room temperature.

Nora's "Sour Cream" Potato Salad

Serves 8

8	russet potatoes, cooked, peeled, and cubed
1 cup	vegan mayonnaise dressing
1 cup	veggie sour cream
¼ cup	pickle relish
¼ cup	diced celery
¼ cup	diced red bell pepper
1 teaspoon	mustard
1 teaspoon	sea salt
Dash of	white pepper
2	garlic cloves, minced
¼ teaspoon	paprika
4 tablespoons	chopped fresh dill

Combine all the ingredients and chill overnight.

Ocean Terrace
Three-Fruit Salad

Serves 6

6	tangerines, peeled and sectioned
1	pineapple, cored and cut into triangles
4	kiwifruit, peeled and cut into wedges
4 teaspoons	light corn syrup
1 bunch	spearmint, leaves only (reserve a few as a garnish)
2 tablespoons	amaretto liqueur
	almond slivers to garnish

Place the fruit in a bowl. Mix the syrup with 4 teaspoons of water and add the mint leaves. Place over heat and stir until the mixture comes to a boil and thickens slightly. Cool and pour the liquid through a strainer to catch the leaves. Pour the liquid over the fruit, sprinkle over the amaretto and toss.

Garnish with almond slivers and mint leaves.

Olive Oyl's Delight

Yields 3½ cups

1 can (6oz)	black olives, drained and chopped
1 jar (6oz)	stuffed green olives, drained and chopped
3	celery ribs, trimmed and diced
¼	yellow bell pepper, diced
2	garlic cloves, minced
1 tablespoon	rice vinegar
2 tablespoons	olive oil

Combine all ingredients and refrigerate overnight.

Swee' Pea Salad

Serves 8 plus

2 cups	vegan mayonnaise dressing
1	large pickle, diced
2 tablespoons	minced onion
1	bell pepper, chopped
½ cup	chopped celery
2 cups	canned peas
2 heads	iceberg lettuce, shredded
2 cups	shredded veggie cheddar
6 tablespoons	smoked tempeh No-Bacos

Mix the vegan mayonnaise dressing, pickle, onion, bell pepper, celery, and peas.

In a 9 x 13-inch serving casserole, or Pyrex dish, layer the lettuce, pea mixture, and cheese. Repeat. Top the final layer of cheese with No-Bacos and refrigerate overnight.

Portobello Mushroom Salad

Serves 2

1	red bell pepper, sliced
1	yellow bell pepper, sliced
1	green bell pepper, sliced
	olive oil
4 teaspoons	chopped basil
	sea salt and pepper
1 tablespoon	chopped tarragon
2	portobello mushrooms
1 cup	veggie feta cheese
2	shallots, chopped
½ cup	sun-dried tomatoes, pureed
4 teaspoons	chopped fresh parsley
4	garlic cloves, minced
2	romaine lettuce leaves

Mix the peppers with some olive oil, the basil, and salt and pepper to taste. Place on a baking sheet and broil for 6 minutes.

Heat some olive oil in a skillet, add the tarragon and mushrooms and sauté for 6 minutes. Combine the cheese, shallots, tomatoes, parsley, and garlic. Spread in between the mushrooms. Place the skillet under a broiler and cook for a further 6 minutes, or until done. Grill the lettuce leaves. Serve the peppers nestled in lettuce, topped with a mushroom and the cheese mixture.

Portobello Potato Salad

Serves 8

6 cups	red potatoes, quartered twice and boiled (with skins)
½ cup	sliced scallions
¼ cup	chopped fresh parsley
4 tablespoons	lemon juice
3 tablespoons	capers, rinsed
3 tablespoons	vegetable broth
2 tablespoons	balsamic vinegar
1 tablespoon	tamari
1 teaspoon	each fresh thyme, oregano, and tarragon
½ teaspoon	pepper
8	garlic cloves, minced
3	portobello mushrooms, thinly sliced

Combine all the ingredients, smashing the red potatoes ever so slightly. Adjust seasoning according to taste. Refrigerate for 2 hours or overnight.

Rajah's Cucumber Salad

Yields 1 cup

1	large cucumber, peeled and diced
1 cup	plain soy yogurt
½ teaspoon	paprika
1 teaspoon	cumin
Dash of	cayenne pepper
Dash of	sea salt
3 tablespoons	chopped fresh mint

Mix all the ingredients together. Serve with curry.

Seize-the-Salad ("Who Made the Salad?")

Serves 4

Croutons:

4 slices	sourdough bread, cut into cubes
4 teaspoons	vegetable margarine
2 teaspoons	Spike
2 tablespoons	grated veggie parmesan

6 cups	torn romaine lettuce
3 tablespoons	olive oil
4 teaspoons	limejuice
1 teaspoon	mustard
1	garlic clove, minced
½ cup	shredded veggie parmesan
	black pepper

First make the croutons. Mix the bread and rest of the crouton ingredients together, place on a cookie sheet and bake at 275°F until cubes are crunchy and browned, about 20 minutes. Cool.

Place the lettuce in a bowl. Place the oil, limejuice, mustard, and garlic in lidded jar and shake well to mix. Pour the dressing over the romaine and toss in the croutons and veggie parmesan. Add pepper to taste.

Smooch Salad

Serves 6

2 cups	arugula
2 cups	spinach
1 cup	dandelion greens
1 cup	enoki mushrooms
12	large strawberries
4 teaspoons	balsamic vinegar
¼ cup	cane sugar
¼ cup	extra virgin olive oil
1 tablespoon	minced scallions
2 tablespoons	sesame seeds, toasted
½ cup	slivered almonds, toasted

Wash, spin and remove the stems from all the greens. Place in a bowl and toss in the mushrooms. Slice the strawberries into "hearts" and add to the greens.

Whisk together the vinegar, sugar, oil, and scallions. Mix in the sesame seeds and pour the dressing over salad. Garnish with almonds.

Stuffed Tomato and Cucumber Salad

Serves 6

6	medium beefsteak tomatoes
6	salad cucumbers, peeled and diced
1 bunch	scallions, thinly sliced
½ cup	green olives, sliced
6 ounces	veggie mozzarella, shredded (reserve a little for garnishing)
½ bunch	cilantro tops, chopped (reserve a little for garnishing)
¼ cup	red wine vinegar
¼ cup	olive oil
Pinch of	sea salt and black pepper
¼	loaf crusty Italian bread, cut into ½-inch cubes

Wash the tomatoes, cut ¼ off the top of each, scoop out the flesh, dice well and set aside. Combine the cucumber, onion, olives, veggie cheese, cilantro, vinegar, oil, and salt and pepper. Mix well and leave to marinate for 15 minutes.

Mix the tomato flesh and bread into the cucumber mixture. Fill the tomatoes with the mixture and serve garnished with several shreds of cheese and a sprig of cilantro.

Summer Fruit Salad

Serves 2

3	plums, peeled and sliced
1	banana, sliced
1 teaspoon	maple syrup
1 teaspoon	balsamic vinegar
¼ teaspoon	nutmeg
2	romaine lettuce leaves

Mix all the ingredients except the lettuce. Pile the mixture onto the lettuce leaves and serve.

Tabbouleh Salad "LaLa Land"

Serves 12

12	medium artichokes
Juice of 1	lemon

Tabbouleh:

1 cup	bulgar
1 cup	boiling water
3	tomatoes, finely chopped
1 cup	finely chopped fresh parsley
¼ cup	finely chopped fresh chives or scallions
¼ cup	finely chopped fresh mint
¼ cup	minced yellow bell pepper
¼ cup	finely chopped black olives
1	cucumber, finely diced

Dressing:

½ cup	limejuice
4 tablespoons	vegetable broth
3 tablespoons	olive oil
3	garlic cloves, minced
¼ teaspoon	cumin
	salt and pepper to taste

Trim and cut off the stems of the artichokes. Place them in boiling water with the lemon juice and cook until tender. Drain then chill. Hollow out the centers.

Mix together the ingredients for the tabbouleh and let it stand 20 minutes. Whisk together the dressing ingredients, pour over the tabbouleh, mix and chill for 2 hours. Serve the tabbouleh in the hollowed out artichokes.

LALA.

Tabbouleh Salad

Serves 4–6

2 cups	boxed couscous, cooked according to directions
½ cup	diced tomato
½ cup	diced cucumber
3 teaspoons	pine nuts
2	garlic cloves, minced
2 tablespoons	olive oil
2 tablespoons	red wine vinegar
	sea salt and pepper to taste

Place the cooked couscous in a bowl. In another bow, mix the tomato, cucumber, and pine nuts with the garlic. Add the oil and vinegar then add the mixture to the couscous. Stir and add salt and pepper. Refrigerate overnight.

Tempeh "No Tuna" Salad

Serves 4

2 cups	tempeh
1½ cups	vegan mayonnaise dressing
½ cup	pickle relish
4 teaspoons	lemon juice
1 teaspoon	fresh dill weed
2	garlic cloves, minced
½ teaspoon	cumin
1	celery rib, diced
3 teaspoons	sunflower seeds, crushed
¼ cup	diced red and green bell peppers
2 teaspoons	finely diced red onion
1	scallion, thinly sliced
4 teaspoons	very finely chopped fresh parsley
2 tablespoons	tamari

Combine all the ingredients and refrigerate for 1 hour.

Serve as a sandwich on bed of lettuce, as a "no tuna" melt etc.

The Light and Loaded
TJ Landing House
Special Salad

Serves 6

The "Light":

½ cup	orange juice
1 teaspoon	maple syrup
1 teaspoon	coconut
1 teaspoon	fennel
½ teaspoon	sea salt
¼ teaspoon	red pepper
½ cup	olive oil

The "Load":

1¼ pounds	fennel bulb, quartered and sliced
2	pears, cored and sliced
2	medium radicchio, sliced
1/4 cup	almond slivers

Whisk the "light" together and toss the "load" together.
Welcome to the Landing!

Veggie Lobster Louie

Serves 4

1	veggie lobster, sliced and diced
½ cup	slivered almonds
½ cup	diced celery
2 tablespoons	fresh dill weed
1 teaspoon	sea salt
½ teaspoon	black pepper
1 cup	diced pineapple
½ teaspoon	cloves
½ teaspoon	cinnamon
2 cups	vegan mayonnaise dressing
1	small butterhead lettuce
	fresh dill weed to garnish

Mix together all the ingredients, except the lettuce and fresh dill. Refrigerate for 3 hours or overnight. Using an ice cream scoop, arrange the mixture on the lettuce leaves and garnish with some dill weed.

Veggie Niçoise Salad

Serves 4

1 cup	veggie tuna, diced
2 teaspoons	tamari
Juice of 1	lemon
½ cup	firm tofu, diced
1 cup	French green beans, cut in half and steamed until al dente
1 bunch	scallions, diced
12	baby roma tomatoes, washed
1	yellow crookneck squash, finely diced
3 tablespoons	capers, well rinsed
1 teaspoon	powdered vegetable seasoning
	salt and pepper
4 cups	arugula

Lemon Vinaigrette:

1 cup	olive oil
1 cup	white wine vinegar
2	garlic cloves, minced
Juice of 1	lemon
3 teaspoons	lemon zest
	salt and pepper to taste

Toss the "tuna" with the tamari. Sprinkle the lemon juice over the tofu and add the vegetable seasoning.

Combine the rest of the salad ingredients then fold in the "tuna" and tofu. Combine the vinaigrette ingredients in a bottle and shake to mix. Pour over the salad and gently mix.

Wake-Me-Up Salad

Serves 6

1	jicama, peeled and cut into 1-inch strips
1	guava, cubed
1	mango, peeled and cubed
¼	pineapple, peeled and cubed
1	small red onion, thinly sliced
1	lime, juiced
1 teaspoon	red-pepper flakes
1 teaspoon	sea salt
1 head	red leaf lettuce, leaves separated

Toss all the ingredients and refrigerate for 1 hour. Serve cold.

Watercress Salad

Serves 4

2 bunches	watercress, trimmed and washed
1	medium jicama, peeled and cut into strips
½ cup	chopped fresh mint (reserve a sprig as a garnish)
¼ cup	olive oil
3 tablespoons	limejuice
¼ teaspoon	sea salt
¼ teaspoon	cracked black pepper
1	avocado, sliced

Combine the watercress, jicama, and mint. Whisk together the oil, limejuice, salt, and pepper. Pour dressing over salad and mix. Garnish with avocado slices and a sprig of mint.

Zesty Coleslaw

Serves 6–8

1 head	white cabbage, thinly sliced
2	carrots, grated
¼ cup	finely diced celery
2	scallions, thinly sliced
1 tablespoon	oregano
1 teaspoon	red pepper
1 teaspoon	powdered vegetable seasoning
1 cup	vegan mayonnaise dressing

Combine the ingredients and refrigerate before serving.

Soups:

CHOOSE FROM HOT OR COLD,

LIGHT OR EARTHY

Combining vegetables, spices and herbs

makes for a tantalizing marriage ...

called soup, wonderful soup!

Almond Cream Soup

Serves 4

5 cups	almond milk
¾ cup	olive oil
6 tablespoons	chopped fresh parsley
2	garlic cloves
4	saffron threads
2 dashes	of sea salt
2 tablespoons	white peppercorns
6 ounces	almond paste
½ cup	cane sugar
	slivered almonds to garnish

In a soup kettle, bring the almond milk to a boil.

Meanwhile, heat the olive oil in a skillet and sauté the parsley, garlic, saffron, salt, and pepper to release their flavors. Place in a food processor and pulse with the almond paste and sugar. Mix the combined ingredients into the milk and simmer an additional 10 minutes.

Garnish with almond slivers.

Artichoke Chowder

Serves 4

4 cups	artichoke hearts, steamed and quartered
4	garlic cloves, minced
½ cup	minced shallots
1 cup	vegetable stock
½ cup	vegetable margarine
4 cups	multigrain milk
	salt and pepper to taste
Sprigs of	basil to garnish
	Herbed Croutons (page 344)

In a skillet, sauté the artichoke hearts, garlic, and shallot in the stock. Set aside half the hearts and puree the rest in a processor. Add the margarine and milk and whip until smooth.

Place in a saucepan and simmer over a low heat for 20 minutes. Season with salt and pepper. Fold in the rest of the hearts and heat thoroughly. Garnish with basil and croutons.

Best Borscht

Serves 8

5	beets, peeled and shredded
2 tablespoons	corn oil
2 teaspoons	white vinegar
8 cups	vegetable broth
2	bay leaves
1 teaspoon	sea salt
1 teaspoon	pepper
3	potatoes, peeled and cubed
2	carrots, peeled and sliced
1 cup	kale, shredded
2 tablespoons	chopped fresh parsley
1	medium yellow onion, chopped
1 tablespoon	flour
1 basket	cherry tomatoes
½ cup	veggie sour cream

Sauté the beets in 1 tablespoon of the oil for 2 minutes; stir in vinegar and set aside.

In a soup pot, place the broth, bay leaves, salt, pepper, potatoes, carrots, kale, and parsley. Bring to a boil, simmer for 30 minutes then add the beets.

Sauté the onion in the rest of the oil for 4 minutes. Whisk in the flour and add the mixture to the soup. Cook until the vegetables are done, 15 minutes or so more. Add the tomatoes and cook 5 minutes more. Process in a food processor, return to the pot, heat then serve. Garnish with "sour cream."

Better-than-Chicken Noodle Soup

Serves 12

3 pounds	veggie chicken, chopped
3 tablespoons	vegetable margarine
	black pepper and sea salt
2	large yellow onions, chopped
3	medium carrots, chopped
2	bay leaves
3	medium celery ribs, chopped
12 cups	vegetable broth
4 ounces	udon noodles, cooked
1 cup	edamame
2 tablespoons	chopped fresh Italian parsley

Place the veggie chicken in a skillet with the margarine and brown it, seasoning to taste with salt and pepper. Put the browned "chicken" into a soup kettle and add the onion, carrots, bay leaves, and celery. Add the vegetable broth to the pot and bring to a boil. Adjust seasonings and simmer for 30 minutes. Add edamame and udon. Simmer until heated through, another 5–7 minutes.

Black Bean Soup

Serves 12

2 cups	black beans, very well rinsed
4 tablespoons	sea salt
2 cups	water
3 tablespoons	olive oil
3	garlic cloves, minced
1 cup	chopped white onion
1 cup	veggie smoked ham
1	large tomato, chopped
4 cups	vegetable broth
2 tablespoons	red wine vinegar
1 teaspoon	cumin
2 teaspoons	black pepper

Place the black beans in a pan with the sea salt and the water and bring to a boil. Reduce the heat and simmer for 2 hours. Sauté the garlic, onion, veggie ham, and tomato in the oil for 5 minutes.

Add the vegetable broth to black beans.

Add vinegar, cumin, and pepper to sauté mixture. Add the sautéed mixture to the black beans and mix. Heat for another 15 minutes.

Cannellini Soupa da Catalina

Serves 6

1 pound	cannellini beans
2 tablespoons	olive oil
2	white onions, chopped
2	garlic cloves, minced
6 cups	vegetable broth
2	bay leaves
2 teaspoons	sea salt
1 teaspoon	black pepper
1 teaspoon	fresh rosemary
6 cups	water
10	carrots, sliced diagonally
1 pound	veggie ham, cut into rounds
1 pound	kale, chopped

In a soup pot, cover the beans with water and soak overnight. The next day, drain, cover with more water, place on top of the stove and bring to a boil. Remove from the heat, let sit one hour then drain.

Heat the oil in skillet, add the onions and garlic and sauté 6 minutes. In a soup pot, place the beans, sautéed onion and garlic, vegetable broth, bay leaves, salt, pepper, and rosemary and cook for 50 minutes, or until the beans are tender. Add 2 cups of water and the carrots.

In a skillet, brown the veggie ham. Add the kale, remaining 4 cups of water, and the veggie ham to soup pot and simmer until the kale is tender, about 15 minutes.

Cheesy Broccoli Bisque

Serves 6

4 cups	broccoli, steamed
1 cup	chopped onion
1 teaspoon	minced garlic
2 tablespoons	olive oil
6 cups	vegetable broth
8 ounces	spaghetti pasta, broken up
6 cups	oat milk
3 cups	shredded veggie cheddar cheese
	salt and pepper

Puree the broccoli and reserve.

In a soup kettle, sauté the onion and garlic in the oil. Add the broth, bring to a boil then add the spaghetti. Boil for 2 minutes then remove the pasta and reserve.

Add the milk and cheese then fold in the broccoli. Heat the soup until the cheese is melted then reintroduce the pasta. Heat thoroughly and season with salt and pepper before serving.

Cream of Hominy Soup

Serves 8

½ cup	hulled pumpkin seeds, toasted
2 cups	tomatillos, cleaned, rinsed, and quartered
8 cups	baby spinach, very well washed
2	chilies, seeded and quartered (jalapeño or serrano)
2 tablespoons	sunflower oil
4 cups	vegetable broth
1	large epazote stem
4 cups	cooked hominy
	salt and pepper

Process the pumpkin seeds then set aside. Place the tomatillos in saucepan with ½ cup of water and cook until soft. Place the tomatillos, spinach, and chilies in a processor with another cup of water and puree until smooth.

Heat the oil in a skillet, add the puree and fry, with the pumpkin seeds, for about 3 minutes. Remove from heat and transfer to a soup kettle. Add the broth and epazote stem and bring to a simmer. Process the hominy, add to the kettle and simmer for 15 minutes longer. Season to taste.

Gazpacho

Serves 6

1½ cups	diced tomatoes
1 cup	diced yellow bell pepper
1 cup	peeled, diced cucumber
¾ cup	diced red onion
2 teaspoons	red wine vinegar
1 teaspoon	tamari
½ teaspoon	black pepper
1 teaspoon	red-pepper flakes
2	garlic cloves, minced
12 ounce	V8 juice
12 ounce	tomato juice
1 cup	avocado slices
1 cup	sliced scallions

Mix all the ingredients except the avocado and scallions. Chill overnight.

Serve garnished with avocado slices and scallions. Tortilla chips are a good accompaniment.

Jazzy French Onion Soup

Serves 8

¼ cup	safflower oil
6 cups	thinly sliced white onion
1 tablespoon	maple syrup
1 teaspoon	white pepper
6 cups	mushroom broth
8	¾-inch slices toasted French bread
½ cup	shredded veggie Swiss cheese
4 teaspoons	grated veggie parmesan

Heat the oil in a soup kettle and add the onions, syrup, and pepper. Cook over a medium heat until the onion is caramelized, about 20 minutes, stirring frequently. Add the broth and bring to a boil. Reduce the heat and simmer for 30 minutes.

Ladle the soup into ovenproof bowls and top with a slice of French bread. Sprinkle the "cheeses" over the top and place under the broiler at 500° F until the "cheese" is melted.

Hot! Hot!

Miso Soup a la Carlsbad

Serves 4

6 cups	water
10 tablespoons	yellow miso
4	scallions, thinly sliced
4 pieces	sea vegetable, cut into pieces
4 ounces	regular tofu, cut into cubes
1 teaspoon	sea salt
2 teaspoons	white pepper

Heat the water until it comes to a boil then slowly add the miso, scallions, and sea vegetable. Stir until the miso paste is dissolved. Add the tofu and simmer for 3 minutes. Add the salt and pepper and serve immediately.

Pappa Al Pomadora

Serves 8

1 cup	olive oil
3	garlic cloves, chopped
½ cup	sage, chopped
8 slices	stale bread, torn or cubed
8 cups	vegetable broth
2 pounds	tomatoes
	sea salt and black pepper

Combine the oil, sage, garlic, and bread. Place on a baking sheet and broil until brown. Place the vegetable broth in a soup pot and bring to a boil.

Puree the tomatoes and put everything into the soup pot. Season with salt and pepper to taste. Simmer for 40 minutes. Great with grilled "cheese"!

Potato and Leek Soup

Serves 4

1	large yellow onion, chopped
¾ cup	chopped leek
3 tablespoons	vegetable margarine
½ teaspoon	sea salt
1 tablespoon	arrowroot
3 cups	oat milk
3	medium white potatoes (2½ cups), peeled, cooked, and cubed
1 tablespoon	minced fresh parsley
1 tablespoon	paprika

Place the onion and leeks in a saucepan with the margarine and sauté until tender, about 5 minutes.

Stir in the salt and arrowroot then gradually add the milk and bring to a boil. Stir for 2 minutes until thickened. Reduce the heat and add the potatoes, parsley, and paprika. Simmer for 10 minutes or until heated through.

Sopa de Albondigas

Serves 12

2 teaspoons	olive oil
½ cup	chopped yellow onion
8 cups	vegetable broth
½ cup	brown rice
2 teaspoons	sea salt
1 teaspoon	pepper
1 teaspoon	coriander
1 teaspoon	cumin
4 tablespoons	fresh mint
4 teaspoons	diced green chilies
2 pounds	veggie meatballs
½ cup	tomato puree

Place the oil and onions in a skillet and sauté. In a stainless steel soup pot, place the broth, rice, seasonings, mint, chilies, and onion. Bring to a boil and then reduce the heat. Add the "meatballs" and tomato puree and simmer for 50–60 minutes, or until the rice is done and the meatballs are tender.

Split Pea Soup

Serves 12

1½ cups	split peas, rinsed and sorted
6 cups	vegetable broth
1	yellow onion, diced
2	yukon gold potatoes, peeled and diced
2	garlic cloves, minced
2	carrots, diced
2 tablespoons	minced fresh cilantro
1 cup	diced veggie ham
	salt and pepper

Place the peas and broth in a soup kettle, bring to a boil then simmer for 1 hour. Add the rest of the ingredients and simmer an hour more. Puree and reheat. Serve with Spicy Soup Croutons (page 345) and a dollop of veggie sour cream.

Tofu Corn Chowder

Serves 12

4 ears	corn, steamed and corn cut off the cob
4 cups	vegetable broth
4 cups	oat milk
2 teaspoons	grated ginger root
2 teaspoons	white pepper
6 tablespoons	tamari
6 teaspoons	soy cream cheese
10-ounce package	tofu, diced
4 tablespoons	shredded bok choy cabbage

Place all the ingredients, except the cream cheese, tofu, and cabbage, in a saucepan. Cook for 15 minutes. Remove the corn and puree in a blender with the soy cream cheese. Return the mixture to the saucepan and allow the soup to thicken.

Add the tofu and simmer until heated through, about 7 minutes or so. Garnish with the bok choy.

Tortilla Soup

Serves 8

2	white onions, finely diced
4	garlic cloves, minced
¼ cup	olive oil
6 cups	vegetable broth
3 cups	Red Salsa (page 329)
1	jalapeño chili, stemmed and seeded
1 bunch	cilantro leaves, very finely chopped
2 teaspoons	sea salt
¾ pound	tortilla chips
½ cup	veggie sour cream
1	avocado, diced
2	limes, cut into 4 wedges each
2 tablespoons	chopped fresh parsley

Sauté the onions and garlic in the olive oil, over a low heat, until caramelized (40 minutes or so). Add the broth, salsa, chili, cilantro, and salt. Simmer for 20 minutes. Add the tortilla chips and cook 10 minutes more, until the chips are softened.

Ladle into bowls and top with a dollop of sour "cream," some diced avocado, a lime wedge, and a sprinkling of chopped parsley.

Truffled Minestrone Soup

Serves 6

4 tablespoons	organic Merlot
2 cups	chopped yellow onion
2	tomatoes, diced
4	carrots, sliced
4	celery ribs, sliced
¼ cup	chopped fresh parsley
4	garlic cloves, minced
1 cup	green lentils
3	bay leaves
5	sprigs thyme
½ sprig	rosemary
10 cups	vegetable broth
	salt and pepper
3 cups	pasta shells
1 bunch	chard, chopped
3 tablespoons	truffle oil

Heat the red wine in a large soup pot, add the onion and sauté until translucent. Add the tomatoes, carrots, celery, parsley, and garlic and cook for 10 minutes, stirring often. Add the lentils, herbs (add to the soup in a bouquet for easy removal) and broth. Bring to a boil and then season to taste. Simmer for 30 minutes.

Remove the herb bouquet and add the pasta and chopped chard. Adjust the seasoning and cook until the pasta is tender, about 10 minutes more. Season each serving of soup with ½ tablespoon of truffle oil.

Vegetable Gumbo Soup

Serves 4

4 cups	vegetable broth
½ cup	long-grain rice
2	large tomatoes, diced
1 tablespoon	olive oil
1	large yellow onion, chopped
3	garlic cloves, minced
½ teaspoon	Gumbo File seasoning
1 pound	okra, sliced
½ teaspoon	powdered vegetable seasoning
	salt and pepper

Place the vegetable broth, rice, and tomato in a soup kettle and bring to a boil.

Heat the oil in a skillet, add the onion and garlic and sauté with the Gumbo File seasoning. Add to the soup. Simmer for 20 minutes, adding the okra and vegetable seasoning during the last 10 minutes. Adjust to taste with salt and pepper.

Vegetable Hot and Sour Soup

Serves 6

5 cups	vegetable broth
¼ cup	rice vinegar
2 tablespoons	cane sugar
¼ teaspoon	cayenne pepper
¼ teaspoon	ground ginger
2 cups	your choice of either veggie shrimp, low mein noodle or your favorite cooked pasta
1½ cups	thinly sliced radish
1½ cups	baby spinach, well washed
¼ cup	thinly sliced scallions

In a large stockpot, bring the vegetable broth to a boil; stir in the vinegar, sugar, cayenne, and ginger. Reduce heat and simmer 5 minutes. Add your choice of ingredient and simmer 5 minutes more. Add the radish, spinach, and scallions. Cover and remove from heat. Allow the soup to stand 4 minutes then serve.

Udon Soup (Kitsune)

Serves 4

6 cups	vegetable broth
3 tablespoons	seaweed powder
1 teaspoon	bonita shavings
1 tablespoon	mirin
1 tablespoon	raw sugar plus 3 tablespoons
¼ cup	light soy sauce or tamari plus 4 tablespoons
4	bean cake pouches (baked tofu)
1 bunch	spinach, very well washed and chopped
4	veggie scallops
4 cups	udon noodles
1	large scallion, thinly sliced

Heat the vegetable broth and add the seaweed powder, bonita, mirin, 1 tablespoon raw sugar, and ½ cup soy sauce. Turn off just before it begins to boil. Cut the bean cake pouches in half and rinse under scalding water to remove excess oil. Add to the broth and allow to rest for 5 minutes. Add the rest of the soy sauce and sugar. Heat for 4 minutes then add the spinach and scallops; continue to simmer while you cook the noodles.

In a separate pot heat some water and add the noodles once the water begins to boil. Cook for 10 minutes on a steady boil, stirring often. Drain.

Once you're ready to serve, place some noodles in each bowl followed by a bean cake. Add the soup broth, and garnish with sliced scallion. Serve immediately—spiced up with chili pepper seasoning!

Wantin' Wonton Soup

Serves 12

Stock:

10 cups	vegetable broth
2 cups	mushrooms, sliced (use several types)
½ bunch	scallions, sliced
1 cup	edamame
4 tablespoons	sesame oil
4 tablespoons	tamari
2 dashes of	sea salt
	sesame oil

Wontons:

2 teaspoons	sesame oil
½ teaspoon	ginger
1	garlic clove, minced
1	medium carrot, shredded
½ cup	water chestnuts, minced
¼ cup	bamboo shoots
½ cup	bean sprouts
1	scallion, minced
3	veggie prawns, minced
¼ cup	veggie chicken, minced
Dash of	sea salt
2 teaspoons	water
2 teaspoons	rice wine
2 teaspoons	tamari
1 teaspoon	arrowroot
24	wonton wrappers

Begin by making the stock. Combine all the ingredients for the stock and slowly simmer 30 minutes to one hour over a medium to low heat. Adjust seasoning to taste.

While the stock is simmering, make the wontons. Heat 1 teaspoon of sesame oil in a wok. Add the ginger, garlic, carrot, water chestnuts, bamboo shoots, and bean sprouts; stir-fry for 2 minutes. Remove the vegetables from the pan. Add more oil and stir-fry the scallion with the veggie prawns and chicken. Add the vegetables and combine. Whisk together the water, wine, tamari, and arrowroot; stir into the vegetables and cook until bubbly, about 2 minutes. Cool. Place 1 teaspoon of mixture in the center of each wonton wrapper and twist the pastry, enclosing or wrapping the filling.

When the wontons are ready, bring the stock to a boil, drop in each wonton and boil 1 minute.

Entrees:

PASTA AND RICE, CURRIES,

STEWS, PIES, FUSION ASIAN,

INDIAN, MEXICAN AND MORE

Is this cookery ... or witchery?

All-Veggie Burritos

Serves 4

4 cups	vegetable broth
1 cup	tomato juice
1	jalapeño chili, seeded and diced
1	large potato, scrubbed and cubed
2	celery ribs, sliced
1	medium zucchini, cubed
1	small onion, chopped
2	carrots, cubed
1 bunch	cilantro, chopped
4 teaspoons	powdered vegetable seasoning
1 tablespoon	pepper
2 teaspoons	arrowroot
4 teaspoons	lime juice
4	large corn tortillas
	Red Salsa or Tomatillo Salsa (pages 329 and 331)
4 tablespoons	shredded lettuce
	Guacamole "Dressing" (page 303)

Place the vegetable broth, tomato juice, chilies, vegetables, and cilantro in a pot, bring to a boil and cook until al dente, about 15 minutes. Drain. Mix in vegetable seasoning, pepper, arrowroot, and lime juice.

Place moistened paper towels between the tortillas and cook in the microwave for 3 minutes. Lay out the tortillas and spread them with the vegetable mixture. Place your choice of 1 teaspoon red salsa or tomatillo salsa over the veggies and 1 tablespoon of shredded lettuce. Fold. Place seam side down in ovenproof pan and heat in a medium oven for 6–10 minutes until heated through.

Serve with Guacamole Dressing and more Red Salsa or Tomatillo Salsa.

Aloo Gobi

Serves 4

3 teaspoons	corn oil
2	chilies, chopped
½ teaspoon	ginger paste
2	garlic cloves, minced
1	yellow onion, chopped
1 teaspoon	cumin
1 teaspoon	cayenne
½ teaspoon	turmeric
1 teaspoon	garam masala powder
½ teaspoon	coriander
	sea salt to taste
1 pound	cauliflower, chopped into 1–2-inch pieces
3	medium potatoes, peeled and chopped into 1–2-inch pieces
	cilantro to garnish

Heat the oil in a skillet and add the chilies, ginger, garlic, and onion and sauté. Add the rest of seasonings, then the cauliflower and potatoes. Sauté 6 minutes then reduce to a simmer and cook until tender. Garnish with cilantro.

This dish is particularly good with Curried Basmati Rice (page 221).

Aviary Ravioli with Hip Herb Pesto

Serves 4

Ravioli:

½ pound	tofu
2 tablespoons	fresh cilantro
1 tablespoon	safflower oil
2 tablespoons	cornstarch
1 tablespoon	egg replacer
1 tablespoon	white wine
¼ teaspoon	grated ginger root
	salt and pepper to taste
1 package	wonton wrappers

Pesto:

½ cup	pine nuts
1 cup	safflower oil
1	jalapeño chili, roasted, skinned, and seeded
4	garlic cloves
1½ cups	fresh basil
½ cup	fresh cilantro
¼ cup	fresh mint
1 tablespoon	maple syrup
Juice of 2	limes
2 tablespoons	tamari

Place all the ravioli ingredients, except the wonton wrappers, in a blender and mix well. Put 1 teaspoon of the mixture onto each wonton wrapper, brush the edges with water and cover with a second wrapper. Press to seal and, if you wish, trim with a decorative cutter. Cover while you prepare the pesto.

Brown the pine nuts in little of the oil. Cool. Place all the pesto ingredients, except the oil, in a food processor and puree until course. Now add the oil a little at a time to adjust pesto moisture. Warm in a saucepan over the stove.

Bring 8 cups of water to a boil and add 1 tablespoon oil. Gently add the ravioli one at a time; once they have popped up to surface, cook an additional minute and then drain.

Serve with the pesto.

California Chili

Serves 8

1	vegan soy hamburger
1	medium onion, chopped
1	green bell pepper, chopped
2 tablespoons	olive oil
3 tablespoons	chopped fresh parsley
3 teaspoons	chili powder
2 teaspoons	sea salt
1 teaspoon	black pepper
1 can (10oz)	kidney beans
1 can (10oz)	chili beans
1 can (24oz)	stewed tomatoes

In a skillet, fry the burger, onions, and bell peppers in olive oil. Add the parsley, salt, and pepper.

In a large saucepan combine the beans, tomatoes, and chili powder. Add the soy hamburger mixture. Simmer until the chili comes to a slow boil, 6 minutes or so. Reduce the heat and simmer on low for 15 minutes.

Caramelized Veggie Scallops with Kiwi Salsa

Serves 4

Kiwi Salsa:

3	kiwifruit, peeled and finely diced
½	small papaya, peeled, seeded, and finely diced
1	large peach, peeled, seeded, and finely diced
1	avocado, peeled, pitted, and diced
½ cup	chopped cilantro
1 tablespoon	limejuice

Scallops:

1	peeled kiwifruit
½ cup	soy yogurt
1	garlic clove, minced
12	veggie scallops
½ cup	hickory syrup

To make the salsa simply combine all the ingredients and refrigerate 2–3 hours. Allow the mixture to come back to room temperature before serving.

To prepare the scallops, puree the kiwifruit, soy yogurt, and garlic; mix well. Marinate the "scallops" in the mixture for 1 hour. Place the syrup in a skillet, add the "scallops" and cook over a medium heat until the syrup is reduced and the scallops are caramelized. Serve with the salsa.

Casa de Granada Hills Baked "Chicken" Breasts

Serves 4

3 cups	picnic barbecue sauce
4	soy chicken breasts
2 tablespoons	sea salt
2 teaspoons	black pepper
1	large yellow onion, sliced
2 cups	chopped bell pepper, green, red, and yellow
8	small red potatoes
2 teaspoons	powdered vegetable seasoning
4 teaspoons	chopped fresh parsley

Pour the barbecue sauce into an ovenproof dish.

Rub the "chicken" with salt and pepper and place in the sauce. Roll over twice to coat the "breasts." Place the onions and bell peppers on top of the breasts. Marinate overnight in the refrigerator.

Preheat the oven to 375°F.

Wash the potatoes and add to dish. Sprinkle the seasoning and parsley over the top and bake for 45 minutes, or until the onions and potatoes are cooked and the "chicken" has browned.

Chili Rellenos

Serves 4

4	large anaheim peppers, roasted, peeled, and seeded
6 ounces	veggie mozzarella cheese, shredded
½ package	vegan taco seasoning mix
3	garlic cloves, minced
½ cup	corn flake crumbles
¼ cup	wheat flour
	egg replacer for 6 eggs
Dash of	salt and pepper
	multigrain milk
2 cups	Rancheros Sauce (page 315) or red enchilada sauce

Preheat the oven to 375°F. Roast the peppers 15 minutes or until the skin blisters. Place in ice water for 2 minutes. Towel dry, and peel off the skin, removing stem and seeds. (Wear gloves!)

Mix the cheese with a quarter package of taco seasoning and the garlic. Combine the corn flakes, flour, egg replacer, salt, pepper, and remaining taco seasoning. Mix in enough milk to make a semi-thick paste.

Stuff the pepper with the cheese mixture and roll in the flour/cornflake mixture, coating well. Lay the peppers on oiled aluminum foil and bake 20 minutes, or until the batter has risen and the coating is browned. Transfer to a baking dish, spoon over the Rancheros Sauce and continue baking until reduced and bubbly, 10 minutes or less.

Great served with a side of Black Beans, Spanish Rice and Guacamole Dressing... "I, Carumba!"

Curried "shrimp"

Serves 6

4 tablespoons	olive oil
3 teaspoons	curry powder
½ teaspoon	red-pepper flakes
½ teaspoon	black pepper
18	veggie prawns
2 cups	vegetable broth
2 tablespoons	tamari
2 cups	fresh wax beans
2 cups	fresh green beans
3 tablespoons	cornstarch

Heat the oil in a skillet. Add the curry powder, pepper, and "shrimp" and sear. Add the broth, tamari, and beans; simmer for 10 minutes.

Mix ¼ cup water with the cornstarch. Add to skillet and simmer, stirring until the sauce thickens. Remove from the heat. Serve over brown rice.

Drunken "shrimp"

Serves 4–6

2 tablespoons	vegetable margarine
½ cup	finely chopped shallots
2 teaspoons	minced garlic
1 tablespoon	minced ginger root
12	veggie shrimp
1 teaspoon	salt
Dash of	black pepper
Dash of	cayenne
1 teaspoon	fresh oregano
1 teaspoon	fresh thyme
Juice of 1	lemon
½ cup	white wine
2 teaspoons	maple syrup
1 cup	almond milk
2 cups	watercress
¼ cup	whiskey
	Herbed Croutons (page 344)

Melt the margarine in a skillet, add the shallot, garlic, and ginger; sauté.

Add the "shrimp" and remaining seasonings, sprinkle with the lemon juice and cook about 3 minutes.

Remove the "shrimp," add the wine and syrup and allow the sauce to reduce. Now add the milk and simmer until thickened again, 5 minutes or so. Place the "shrimp" on a bed of watercress and sprinkle with whiskey. Pour the sauce over the shrimp and arrange croutons around the plate.

East Meets West Spaghetti

Serves 4

½ cup	olive oil
10	garlic cloves, minced
1 pound	sliced shiitake mushrooms
1 bunch	scallions, sliced
2 tablespoons	tamari
	sea salt
	white pepper
1 pound	thin spaghetti

Place the olive oil and garlic in a skillet, add the mushrooms and sauté until crispy. Add scallions, tamari, and salt and pepper to taste.

Cook the pasta according to package directions. Drain and rinse in cold water then rinse in boiling water.

Combine the pasta and sauce. Serve with fresh crusty bread.

Eggplant "Parmesan"

Serves 4

¼ cup	olive oil
½ cup	veggie parmesan cheese
1 cup	bread crumbs
2 tablespoons	dried basil, crushed
2 tablespoons	dried parsley, crushed
1 teaspoon	sea salt
1 teaspoon	pepper
8 tablespoons	vegan mayonnaise dressing
1	medium eggplant, cut into ½-inch thick slices
4 tablespoons	veggie romano and parmesan shreds

Preheat oven to 375°F. Oil a cookie sheet with olive oil.

In a medium mixing bowl, combine ½ cup parmesan cheese, the bread crumbs, basil, parsley, salt, and pepper.

Spread the "mayo" on both sides of each eggplant slice. Now coat the eggplant slices in the breadcrumb mixture and place on the cookie sheet. Bake for 20 minutes.

Sprinkle the shredded "cheese" over the eggplant slices and bake until just melted.

Exotic Grilled Veggies

Serves 4

4 cups	balsamic vinegar
2–4 pieces each:	
	romaine lettuce or endive
	artichoke heart
	anise or fennel
	eggplant
	zucchini
	portobello mushroom
	yam
	red onion

Place the balsamic vinegar in a saucepan and boil until reduced by half.

Heat the grill, place the veggies over the hot coals and sear for 4–5 minutes, brushing them with balsamic vinegar as they are turned.

Falafel and New Potatoes in Saffron Gravy

Serves 6

1 package	falafel vegetarian patty mix
¼ cup	olive oil
2 pounds	baby new potatoes
4	garlic cloves, minced
4 tablespoons	tamari
1 cup	tahini paste
10 ounces	tofu
Dash of	pepper
Juice of 1	lemon
1	saffron thread
¾ cup	vegetable broth

Prepare the falafel according to package directions, but form into balls rather than patties. Fry in olive oil.

Boil the new potatoes. Drain and coat with oil, half the minced garlic, and 2 teaspoons tamari. Combine with the falafel balls and reserve in the skillet.

Puree the tahini, rest of tamari, remaining garlic, tofu, pepper, and lemon juice.

In a skillet sear the saffron thread with the vegetable broth. Slowly add the puree and bring to a boil then reduce to a simmer. Add the falafel and potatoes. Simmer together for 15 minutes.

Gimme Gyoza...
Down-Sized!

Serves 8

½ cup	diced carrots
½ cup	thinly sliced cabbage
½ cup	mung bean sprouts
½ cup	thinly sliced scallion
1 block	firm tofu
2	garlic cloves, minced
1 tablespoon	toasted sesame oil
1 teaspoon	tamari
1 package	wonton wrappers
	safflower oil
¼ cup	vegetable broth

Blanch the vegetables in boiling water for 30 seconds. Chill, squeezing out excess water.

Puree the tofu in a blender. Add the vegetables and seasonings and pulse, removing any large chunks. Fill the wrappers with one teaspoon of filling per wonton. Fold and crimp.

In a skillet, heat 2 tablespoons oil; place gyoza in pan and cook 4 minutes to brown the bottoms. Add the vegetable broth, cover and allow them to steam for about 5 minutes until firm.

Serve with dipping sauce (try a mixture of tamari, rice wine vinegar, sesame seeds, and scallion).

Ginger Snow Peas with Lemon Vermicelli

Serves 4

1 pound	vermicelli
¼ cup	lemon juice
6 tablespoons	olive oil
1 teaspoon	coriander
½ teaspoon	ginger
¾ pound	snow peas, julienne cut
1 cup	white wine
1 cup	enoki mushrooms
Dash of	sea salt
1 tablespoon	lemon zest
4 tablespoons	basil pesto
	fresh basil to garnish

Cook the pasta. Drain and rinse. Add the lemon juice.

Heat 3 tablespoons of the oil in a skillet, add the spices and sear them. Quickly add the snow peas and stir-fry. Add the wine and reduce, allowing the sauce to thicken. Once thickened, add mushrooms and salt. Cook 1 minute longer.

In another skillet heat the remaining oil and add the vermicelli. Cook, lightly stir-frying, for 3 minutes. Toss with the zest.

Serve the snow peas over the vermicelli, garnished with a sprig of basil.

Great White Bean Quesadillas

Serves 4

1 cup	great northern beans, cooked and drained
½ teaspoon	cumin
8	large flour tortillas
4 teaspoons	chopped pickled jalapeños
½ cup	green chilies
¼ cup	refried black beans
8 slices	tomato
¾ cup	shredded veggie cheese
4 teaspoons	chopped cilantro
	olive oil or cooking spray
8 ounces	veggie sour cream

In a bowl, combine the beans with the cumin.

Place ¼ cup of beans on four of the tortillas; mash into the surface. Divide equally and layer jalapenos, chilies, and black beans on top. Top with tomato slices, cheese, and cilantro. Top with remaining 4 tortillas and lightly brush with olive oil. Place in oven at 375° F and bake until crispy light brown.

Slice each tortilla into quarters and serve with veggie sour cream.

Green Lasagna

Serves 8 plus

1 pound	lasagna noodles
3 tablespoons	olive oil
3 bunches	spinach, very well washed
1 cup	tofu
1 cup	veggie cream cheese
8	garlic cloves, minced
½ teaspoon	nutmeg
1¼ teaspoons	sea salt
1 teaspoon	black pepper
2 cups	broccoli florets, blanched
3 cups	Faux Béchamel Sauce (page 310)
3 cups	Red Sauce ... for Pasta (page 316)
2 cups	veggie Parmesan
¼ cup	chopped fresh chives

Cook the noodles according to package directions then lay out and brush with oil.

Put the spinach, tofu, cream cheese, garlic, nutmeg, salt, and pepper in food processor and mix well. Fold in the blanched broccoli florets.

Preheat the oven to 350° F. Oil a 9 x 13 inch baking dish and assemble the lasagna in the following order: noodles, red sauce, green and "cheese" mixture, béchamel sauce, veggie parmesan. Repeat 2–3 times more and sprinkle "cheese" and chives over the final top layer of béchamel sauce. Bake, covered, for 30 minutes then uncover for an additional 5 minutes. Allow the lasagna to sit at least 10 minutes prior to serving.

Can be served garnished with additional broccoli florets.

Grilled Tofu and Vegetables

Serves 6

10-ounce	slab firm tofu, cut in half, then twice more to make 6 "steaks"
2 cups	Sweet Miso Sauce (page 317)
8 tablespoons	cooking sherry
8 tablespoons	liquid smoke
4 tablespoons	olive oil
2 teaspoons	red-pepper flakes
1 teaspoon	sea salt
4 teaspoons	chopped fresh golden sage
1	medium Japanese eggplant, sliced lengthwise and into 6 pieces
1 bunch	scallions, trimmed
1	medium zucchini, sliced lengthwise into 6 pieces
6	small new potatoes
1	leek, trimmed and sliced lengthwise (discard greens) into 6 pieces
3	medium tomatoes, sliced in half
2 ears	white corn, shucked and sliced into 3 pieces

Marinate the tofu in the hickory miso sauce for 12 hours, turning twice.

Mix together the sherry, smoke, oil, red-pepper flakes, salt, and sage. Place the vegetables in dish and marinate in the sherry mixture for 12 hours.

Grill the vegetables over hot coals, brushing with marinade until done (approximately 15–20 minutes). Grill the tofu steaks over hot coals until grill marks appear and the tofu is heated through, 5–7 minutes. Heat the hickory miso sauce and serve with the tofu and vegetables.

Hawaiian "Chicken"

Serves 8

1 pound	veggie chicken
4 tablespoons	olive oil
3	garlic cloves, minced
1	medium yellow onion, chopped
½	each yellow, red and green bell pepper, sliced lengthwise and chopped
½	fresh pineapple, sliced into 1-inch pieces
3 tablespoons	tamari
1 teaspoon	black pepper
1 teaspoon	powdered vegetable seasoning
2 cups	vegetable broth
2 teaspoons	cornstarch

Place the "chicken" in a skillet coated with 3 tablespoons of olive oil. Add garlic and cook until the "chicken" is browned, about 4 minutes per side. Remove from the heat and set aside. Wipe skillet and add the remaining oil. Add the onions and peppers; cook for 3 minutes. Now add the "chicken," tamari, pepper, vegetable seasoning, and pineapple. Slowly add the vegetable broth and heat until gently boiling.

Remove ½ cup broth from the pan, allow to cool then combine with the cornstarch. Add to the skillet and stir constantly until the sauce thickens. Reduce heat to low and simmer an additional 3–5 minutes.

Serve over your choice of brown or white rice.

Holiday Wraps

Serves 4

4	large collard greens
2	garlic cloves, minced
½ teaspoon	black pepper
4	vegan soy turkey breasts, split in half
1 cup	crushed pineapple
½ quantity	Cornbread Stuffing recipe (page 227)
1 bunch	red chard, washed and torn
2 tablespoons	vegetable margarine
1	lemon
1 cup	organic Chardonnay

Preheat the oven to 350°F.

Boil the collard leaves in water for 10 minutes and pat dry.

Spread the garlic and pepper over the soy turkey. Place the pineapple in a skillet and heat. Once the pan is hot add the "turkey" and flash cook. Mound the stuffing into the split breasts, to resemble a sandwich. Place each filled breast on a collard leaf and roll, wrapping as you fold.

Parboil the red chard in boiling water for 8 minutes. Drain.

Grease an ovenproof baking dish with the margarine. Place the red chard evenly in the dish and nestle the wraps on top. Pour the Chardonnay over the top and squeeze fresh lemon juice over the top.

Bake for 30 minutes, or until the wine has reduced and the wraps are steamy and tender. Serve over the chard.

Hungarian Stroganoff

Serves 4

2 cups	vegetable broth
4 cups	spinach or tomato fettuccini
1 cup	multigrain milk
3 tablespoons	ketchup
Dash of	salt and pepper
	olive oil
1 cup	thinly sliced red onions
8	garlic cloves, minced
3 tablespoons	caraway seed
6	roma tomatoes, chopped
1 cup	fresh basil, chopped
½ cup	white wine
1 cup	veggie Caraway Jack, cubed
	pepper to taste

Bring the broth to a boil, add the pasta and cook until a la dente, 7 minutes or so. Remove from the heat and drain, retaining broth.

Add the milk and ketchup to the broth and season.

Heat the olive oil in a skillet, add the onion, then garlic and caraway seed. Add tomatoes and basil, pour in wine and cook until reduced, about 10 minutes. Add the "cheese" and milk mixture, bring to a boil then reduce heat, simmering an additional 6 minutes. Add the pasta and pepper then serve.

"Kitchen Sink" Veggie Enchiladas

Serves 6

6	ancho chilies, stemmed and seeded
1	large red onion, chopped
4	garlic cloves, minced
¼ cup	corn oil
1 teaspoon	cumin
½ cup	tamari
2½ cups	water
8 teaspoons	whole-wheat flour
1½ cups	assorted vegetables/tofu (leftovers)
1 teaspoon	sea salt
12	large corn tortillas and 1 teaspoon corn oil
1 cup	cheddar veggie shreds

Preheat the oven to 350°F.

Roast the chilies under a broiler until the skins blister. Rinse in cold water and chop fine.

Sauté the onion and garlic in oil. Add the chilies, cumin, tamari, and water. Bring to a boil, then reduce the heat; remove ¼ cup of liquid, mix with the flour and return it to the pot. Simmer 8 minutes to allow the sauce to thicken.

Pick your choice of vegetables—whatever is in the refrigerator or even last night's leftover mashed potatoes and corn, tofu, etc*. Dice small. Steam the vegetables, either in a steamer or in a bag in the microwave; toss with sea salt.

Oil a steamer or double boiler with the reserved teaspoon of corn oil and steam the tortillas 60–90 seconds.

Fill each tortilla with the vegetable/tofu/leftovers mixture and roll. Place, seam side down, in an oiled ovenproof baking dish. Spread the sauce over tortillas then sprinkle over the cheese.

Bake 20 minutes or until heated through and the cheese has melted. Serve with Tomatillo Salsa (page 331).

* You can substitute more "cheese" for the leftovers if you like.

Kofta and Gravy

Serves 2

Koftas:

2 cups	mixed carrot, cauliflower and potatoes, boiled
¾ teaspoon	ginger
2 tablespoons	flour
	sea salt and black pepper to taste
8 tablespoons	safflower oil

Gravy:

4 tablespoons	safflower oil
1 cup	boiled onions, pureed
1 cup	diced tomatoes
3	bay leaves
1 teaspoon	ginger paste
2	garlic cloves, minced
½ teaspoon	diced chili
1 teaspoon	chili powder
¾ teaspoon	turmeric
1 teaspoon	garam masala
	sea salt and pepper
½ cup	almond milk
	coriander to garnish

Mash the veggies with the ginger, flour, and salt and pepper to taste. Form the mixture into balls. Heat the oil in a skillet and fry the koftas until browned; drain on paper towels.

Heat the oil for the gravy in a saucepan and add all the gravy ingredients, except the milk and coriander, one at a time. Heat for 3 minutes. Now add the milk, allow the mixture to thicken to a gravy and cook for about 5 minutes. Add the kofta balls and heat for 3 minutes. Garnish with chopped coriander.

Kung POW! Tofu

Serves 4

1 cup	tamari
½ cup	hickory syrup
3	garlic cloves, chopped
1 teaspoon	black pepper
2 teaspoons	red-pepper flakes
2 tablespoons	grated ginger root
1 bunch	scallions, sliced
12-ounce package	firm tofu, sliced into cubes and patted dry
4 tablespoons	olive oil
½ teaspoon	sea salt
¼ cup	each sliced green, red, and yellow bell pepper
1 cup	roasted cashews

Mix together the tamari, syrup, garlic, black and red peppers, ginger root, and scallions. Add the tofu and leave to marinate for 24 hours.

Heat the oil in a skillet, add the salt and tofu, and fry until the tofu is crisp; drain on paper towels. Wipe the skillet, add the marinade and sauté the bell peppers in the mixture for 4 minutes. Add the cashews and tofu. Cook an additional 4 minutes.

Great with Sticky Rice (page 226).

Mary's Veggies and "Catch de Jour" with Lemon Garlic Sauce

Serves 6

3 cups	all-purpose flour
3 tablespoons	paprika
1 teaspoon	onion powder
1 teaspoon	garlic powder
½ teaspoon	each fresh sage, oregano, and thyme
	salt and pepper
1	beet, sliced
6	asparagus spears
1	yam, peeled and sliced
½	bell pepper, sliced
1	fennel bulb, quartered
12	veggie shrimp
	vegetable oil

Lemon Garlic Sauce:

½ block	tofu
1 tablespoon	Dijon mustard
3	garlic cloves
Juice of 1	lemon
½ teaspoon	salt
¾ cup	olive oil
¼ cup	extra virgin olive oil
	cayenne pepper

Mix the flour, paprika, onion and garlic powders, herbs, salt, and pepper. Dredge the veggies and "shrimp" in the mixture. Fry in oil until crisp and golden, 3–4 minutes. Drain on paper towels.

Put the tofu, mustard, garlic, lemon juice, and salt in blender and mix; slowly add the oil. Heat as a fondue or sauce on the side and sprinkle with cayenne ... a Portuguese tempura of sorts.

Merlot Bell Peppers

Serves 4

4	bell peppers, any color
2 teaspoons	olive oil
½ pound	vegan soy hamburger
2	garlic cloves, minced
4 tablespoons	chopped fresh parsley
¼ cup	chopped black olives
¼ cup	fresh corn
6 tablespoons	capers
3 cups	bread crumbs
4 teaspoons	vegetable margarine, melted
1 cup	organic Merlot
	salt and pepper to taste

Remove the cores from the bell peppers and wash. Pat dry. Preheat oven to 375° F.

Heat the olive oil in a skillet, add the burger, garlic, and parsley and fry. When the burger mixture is brown add the olives, corn, and capers. Work in the bread crumbs and melted margarine.

Score the bell peppers then stuff with the mixture. Place in an oiled ovenproof baking dish. Pour the Merlot over the peppers and season. Bake 30 minutes, or until browned and the liquid is reduced—the pepper skins will blister.*

*For an added flavor, try sprinkling veggie parmesan on the peppers just before serving.

Midwest-Style Veggie Chops and Brown Rice

Serves 6

6	celery ribs, trimmed and sliced into ½-inch pieces
6	carrots, trimmed and sliced into ½-inch pieces
¼ cup	chopped yellow onion
1 tablespoon	tamari
1½ cups	brown rice, washed
4 teaspoons	olive oil
3 tablespoons	chopped fresh parsley
6	wheat gluten cutlets
½ cup	organic red wine

Parboil the celery and carrots in 4 cups of salted water until tender, about 15 minutes. Drain off and reserve the vegetable broth. Bring reserved broth, onion, and tamari to a boil in a stainless steel pot. Add brown rice. Cover pot and again bring to a boil. Reduce heat to medium and cook 30 minutes.

Heat the oil in a skillet, add the parsley; sear. Add the cutlets and cook until brown, about 2 minutes each side. Add the wine, celery, carrots, and rice. Simmer all the ingredients together on low heat an additional 10 minutes, or until the wine is absorbed.

Minced Squab—Not! (Chinese Tacos)

Serves 8-12

3 tablespoons	peanut oil
1 pound	veggie chicken, diced very small OR
	1 pound firm tofu, diced very small
2	garlic cloves, grated
1 bunch	scallions, thinly sliced
1 teaspoon	grated ginger root
½ cup	diced bamboo shoots
1 cup	water chestnuts, diced
1	large carrot, grated
8	Chinese black mushrooms, minced
1 cup	vegetable broth
3 tablespoons	lite soy sauce
3 tablespoons	sake or sherry
1 teaspoon	cane syrup
1 teaspoon	cornstarch
8-12	iceberg lettuce leaves
½ cup	chopped peanuts

Heat the peanut oil in a large wok. Add the veggie chicken or tofu and stir-fry quickly with garlic and scallion. Add the ginger root, bamboo shoots, water chestnuts, carrot, mushroom, and broth. Cook for 3 minutes or so until the broth is reduced by 90 percent.

In a separate bowl, whisk the soy sauce, sake or sherry, and syrup with the cornstarch. Stir into the "chicken" mixture and cook until it boils; remove from heat.

Fill a lettuce leaf, sprinkle with peanuts, and drizzle some sauce over the top ... ah so!

Miso Marinated "Fish" with Baby Bok Choy

Serves 4

1 cup	white miso
2 teaspoons	black pepper
1 teaspoon	grated ginger root
1 cup	mirin
2 tablespoons	tamari
1	large veggie fish, cut into 8 x 2-inch slices
4	baby bok choy
Juice of 1	lemon and 1 teaspoon zest
1 teaspoon	toasted sesame seed
4 tablespoons	sesame oil

Mix miso, pepper, ginger root, mirin, and tamari. Place the "fish" in the marinade and allow to sit overnight. Reserve the marinade.

Preheat the oven to 325° F. Place the "fish" in parchment, wrap, and place on a rack over a baking dish containing 2 cups of water. Place the bok choy in the water. Bake for 15 minutes on the highest rack of the oven, turning the "fish" and cabbage once. Remove the bok choy, sprinkle with lemon and sesame. Serve the "fish" alongside with warm reserved marinade. Great with steamed rice.

Nina's Vegan Spaghetti

Serves 6

6 tablespoons	olive oil
6 tablespoons	chopped fresh basil
2 tablespoons	chopped fresh oregano
½ tablespoon	chopped fresh rosemary
1 teaspoon	sea salt
1 teaspoon	black pepper
3	garlic cloves, minced
1 cup	white mushrooms, sliced
½ cup	canned button mushrooms
1 cup	chopped yellow, red, green bell peppers
12 ounces	canned stewed tomatoes
2 cups	vegetable broth
2 cups	organic Chardonnay
1 pound	thin spaghetti

Heat 4 tablespoons of the olive oil in a skillet. Add the herbs, spices, garlic, mushrooms, and peppers; cook for 6 minutes. Add the tomatoes, broth, and wine and simmer for 20 minutes.

Bring water and 2 tablespoons olive oil to a boil, add the pasta and cook for 3 minutes. Remove from the heat and drain. Rinse in cold water, followed by hot. Place in a serving dish and mix with the sauce.

Old-Fashioned Salisbury Steak...NOT!

Serves 6

	safflower oil
8 slices	veggie bacon
1	yellow onion, chopped
2	soy hamburgers, crumbled
6	garlic cloves, chopped
3 tablespoons	Dijon mustard
6 teaspoons	egg replacer
	sea salt
	black pepper
3	shallots, minced
2 cups	mushrooms, sliced
½ cup	wheat flour or bread crumbs
1 teaspoon	thyme
½ teaspoon	fresh rosemary
¼ cup	almond milk
2 cups	organic Merlot

Preheat the oven to 375°F.

Place 1–2 teaspoons of oil in a skillet, add the veggie bacon and fry. Remove from the heat and pat dry between paper towels. In a processor, blend the "bacon" and onion to a purée.

Place the crumbled "hamburger" in a mixing bowl and mix in the garlic, mustard, and onion purée. Slowly add the egg replacer; season to taste. Form into 6 large "steaks."

Reheat the skillet, add the shallots and steaks and brown on both side. Remove and transfer to an oiled ovenproof dish.

Heat 2 teaspoons of oil in the skillet, sauté the mushrooms then stir in the flour, herbs, and milk. Season with salt and pepper, add the Merlot, and mix well. Pour the sauce over the veggie steaks. Bake for 20 minutes until bubbly.

Serve with your favorite vegetable, Smashed Potatoes (page 216) and World's Best Veggie Gravy (page 321).

Paella Number 501

Serves, generously, 4–6

¼ cup	olive oil
1½ cups	basmati rice
½ pound	vermicelli
1	yellow onion, chopped
2	garlic cloves, minced
¼ teaspoon	marjoram
1 package	veggie chicken nuggets
1 pound	veggie prawns, chopped
1 pound	veggie salmon
1 package	veggie scallops
2 threads	saffron
½ each	red, yellow, green bell pepper
½ pound	snap peas
4	tomatoes, sliced
1 teaspoon	sea salt
1 teaspoon	black pepper
1 cup	vegetable broth

Heat the oil in a large paella pan and add the rice, vermicelli, onion, garlic, and marjoram. Heat until the onion is lightly brown.

Add the veggie meats and saffron and brown a little. Add the peppers, peas, tomatoes, salt, and pepper. Slowly add the broth and simmer gently for 25 minutes, covered, to allow the rice to cook.

Pasta Primavera 1998 (Blue Parrot)

Serves 8

2 tablespoons	olive oil
2-pound package	penne pasta
½ cup	olive oil
1 head	garlic, minced
2 teaspoons	sea salt
1 teaspoon	white pepper
3 tablespoons	chopped fresh sage
1	each green, yellow, and red bell pepper, julienne cut
½ cup	broccoli florets
4	carrots, julienne cut
½ cup	thinly sliced red onion
1 tablespoon	grated lemon peel
6 tablespoons	grated veggie parmesan cheese sage sprig to garnish

Add the 2 tablespoons of olive oil to a pan of water, add pasta and cook according to instructions. Drain, rinse, and cover with cold water for 10 minutes.

Heat the oil in a skillet and add the garlic, salt, pepper, sage, and vegetables; sauté until al dente, about 3 minutes. Add the lemon peel, mix well, and simmer 2 minutes more. Remove from the heat.

Drain the pasta and rinse under boiling water. Drain and place in pasta dish. Mix in the vegetables, coating well. Sprinkle with grated parmesan and garnish with a sage sprig.
Serve with breadsticks.

Personal Pizzas

Serves 10

4 cups	white or whole-wheat flour
4 cups	cold water
3 packages	active yeast
½ cup	cane sugar

Place the flour on a board, make a hole in the center and fill with water. Add the yeast. Mix slowly with wooden spatula and once mixed, work with your hands. Mix the sugar in. Roll, work, and roll. Allow the dough to rest for 2–3 minutes in between working it. Roll into a sausage shape and cut into 10 slices.

Take each slice and roll out using a rolling pin. Place the crusts on oil-coated aluminum foil and stack. You can now either refrigerate them or freeze them until ready for use.

These are a great "pizza party" idea as guests can create their own toppings!

Pesto El Burro

Serves 6

1 pound	thin spaghetti
4 teaspoons	olive oil
2 cups	fresh basil, chopped
1 bunch	fresh parsley, chopped
	sea salt to taste
	black pepper to taste
1 cup	shredded veggie mozzarella
1 cup	grated veggie parmesan

Cook the spaghetti according to package instructions then rinse in cold water.

Heat the oil in a skillet and add the basil, parsley, and seasoning. Sear then remove from the heat. Mix in the shredded "mozzarella" and allow it to melt.

Rinse the spaghetti in boiling water and add the cheese mixture. Toss in the veggie parmesan and serve immediately.

Piedmont Pepper UnSteak

Serves 6

6	veggie pepper steaks
2	carrots, peeled and grated
1	medium onion, thinly sliced
2	celery ribs, thinly sliced
½ cup	chopped fresh Italian parsley
2	bay leaves
1 teaspoon	peppercorns
2 cups	organic red wine
1 tablespoon	vegetable margarine
	sea salt
2 tablespoons	olive oil

Combine all the ingredients, except the oil, and marinate for 24 hours. Preheat the oven to 350°F.

Heat the oil in a skillet, add the "steak" and fry until browned; pat dry. Place the marinade in an ovenproof baking dish. Return the steaks to the marinade. Baste well each side and season with salt to taste. Bake for 20 minutes.

Pierogis

Serves 4

1 cup	flour
1 teaspoon	olive oil
¼ cup	vegetable broth
3	medium potatoes, cubed
1	medium yellow onion, chopped (OR 2 cups spinach and 2 small shallots OR 2 cups kale and ½ cup red onion)
2	garlic cloves
1 teaspoon	fresh chives (dill if you use the spinach and parsley if you use the kale)
1 teaspoon	vegetable margarine
½ cup	multigrain milk
½ teaspoon	sea salt
½ teaspoon	pepper

Combine the flour, oil, and broth. Roll out on a floured surface and cut into 3-inch diameter rounds.

Boil the potatoes until tender. In a skillet, sauté the onion and garlic with the chives in a ½ teaspoon olive oil (or spinach, shallot, garlic, and dill; or kale, red onion, garlic, and parsley). Combine the potatoes, onion mixture, margarine, and milk; whip until creamy. Add the salt and pepper.

Place 1 tablespoon of the potato mixture on each dough round and fold over, crimping the edges together. Place in boiling water and cook until each pierogis pops to the surface. Ladle into a skillet and fry with olive oil, browning each side.

Serve with veggie sour cream as a side dish or with a white or red sauce as an entrée.

Pink Citrus " Fish"

Serves 4

Citrus Wine Sauce:

¼ cup	organic white wine
2 tablespoons	white wine vinegar
1	shallot, minced
3	pink grapefruit, peeled and sectioned
½ cup	vegetable margarine
	salt and pepper

"Fish":

2	veggie fish, cut in half
2 teaspoons	red pepper
2 tablespoons	olive oil
1 pound	fresh shiitake mushrooms, sliced
1	red and 1 white endive, cut crosswise

In a saucepan, place the wine, vinegar, shallot, and grapefruit sections (reserve 1 tablespoon peel and 1 cup sections). Pulverize the grapefruit in the sauce. Boil the sauce until reduced to 1 tablespoon then add the margarine a little at a time and allow it to melt into the sauce before adding each piece. Season with salt and pepper. Set aside.

Heat the oil in a skillet, add the "fish" and red pepper and fry. Set aside. Sauté the mushrooms and endive for about 1 minute. Add the 1 cup fruit segments and spoon onto plates. Top with the "fish," drizzle the citrus wine sauce over the food and garnish with zest.

Pizzeria Veggie Loaf

Serves 12

2 pounds	vegan soy hamburger
2 slices	wheat bread
	egg replacer for 1 egg
½ cup	vegetable broth
3	garlic cloves, minced
½	onion, minced
1 teaspoon	each fresh basil, oregano, and thyme
	salt and pepper
1 cup	veggie pepperoni
½ cup	black olives, chopped
½ cup	chopped bell pepper
1	zucchini, shredded
1	carrot, shredded
2 cups	veggie mozzarella, shredded
1 quantity	Red Sauce ... for Pasta recipe (page 316)

Preheat the oven to 350°F.

Mix the soy burger, wheat bread, egg replacer, broth, garlic, onion, spices, salt, and pepper. Form into a flat rectangular block about 12 x 8 inches and about ½-inch thick. Layer the veggie pepperoni, olive, bell pepper, zucchini, carrot, and "cheese" over the top. Press down. Start at one end and roll, creating a loaf. Place in greased loaf pan and pour the Red Sauce over the top. Bake, uncovered, for about 30 minutes until bubbly.

Potato Chimichangas

Serves 8*

2	medium potatoes, peeled, quartered, and cooked
2 cups	black beans, cooked
½ cup	vegetable broth
2	jalapeño chilies, washed, seeded, and chopped
2 tablespoons	tamari
8	wheat tortillas
1 cup	safflower oil

Mash the potatoes and black beans together, adding the broth, chilies, and tamari.

Lay a tortilla out, fold half the tortilla toward the center then repeat for other side. Now place ⅛ of the filling at one end of the folded tortilla and roll. Repeat with the remaining tortillas and filling.

Place the oil in a skillet or deep fryer, add the tortillas, seam side down, and fry until brown and crispy. Drain very well on paper towels.

Serve with Guacamole "Dressing," Red Salsa, or Tomatillo Salsa (pages 303, 329, and 331).

*This recipe can also be served as an appetizer for 16—simply cut the chimichangas in two.

Potato Curry

Serves 6

4	large potatoes, peeled and cubed
½ cup	corn oil
2	chili peppers, chopped
1 teaspoon	curry powder
2 teaspoons	cumin
½ teaspoon	sea salt
3 teaspoons	tomato paste
½ teaspoon	mustard seeds
1 teaspoon	lemon juice
5 teaspoons	chopped coriander

Boil the potatoes until tender then drain. Heat the oil in a saucepan, add the peppers, curry powder, cumin, salt, tomato paste, and mustard seeds; sear for 1 minute. Add the potatoes then gradually stir in the lemon juice and coriander. Heat thoroughly. Serve with a rice dish of your choice.

Roasted "Chicken" with Apple Crème Sauce

Serves 4

¼ cup	minced white onion
4 tablespoons	vegetable margarine
1 cup	bread crumbs
¼ cup	diced apple
1 tablespoon	chopped fresh parsley
3 tablespoons	chopped pecans
	salt and pepper to taste
4	veggie chicken breasts, split in half
4	veggie bacon strips
	olive oil
½ cup	apple liqueur
½ cup	vegetable broth
½ cup	almond milk
2 tablespoons	arrowroot

Preheat the oven to 395°F. Sauté the onion in 2 tablespoons of the margarine. Add the remaining margarine, the breadcrumbs, apples, parsley, pecans, salt, and pepper. Combine well.

Stuff the 4 "breasts" with the mixture. Secure them by tying a strip of uncooked veggie bacon around the middle. Brush with olive oil and place in an oiled ovenproof baking dish.

In a saucepan combine the apple liqueur, broth, and almond milk. Bring to a boil and remove 3 tablespoons of the mixture. Allow it to cool then add the arrowroot; combine and return the mixture to the saucepan. Stir until thickened and remove from the heat. Pour over the stuffed breasts and roast for 20 minutes. Serve over a bed of Blow Me Down! Lemon Spinach (see page 194).

Sauerkraut and 'WheatBraten"

Serves 6

4 teaspoons	olive oil
1 pound	wheat chicken
1 teaspoon	cumin
1 teaspoon	powdered vegetable seasoning
1 tablespoon	whole peppercorns
6	medium potatoes, peeled and quartered
¼ cup	white wine vinegar
2 cups	sauerkraut

Heat the oil in a skillet, add the wheat chicken, cumin,
vegetable seasoning, and peppercorns and cook until browned.
Remove from the heat.

Place the potatoes in bottom of a Dutch oven. Add
6 tablespoons of water and the vinegar. Layer "chicken"
on top and follow with the sauerkraut. Cover, bring to a boil
over medium heat, and then simmer until the potatoes are
tender, about 30 minutes.

Serve with margarine and brown mustard.

Savory Shepherd's Pie

Serves 4

5 teaspoons	vegetable margarine
½ cup	sliced onion
½ cup	red bell pepper
½ cup	thinly sliced parsnips
3 teaspoons	savory
2	garlic cloves, minced
½ teaspoon	sea salt
1 teaspoon	black pepper
1 cup	veggie mutton
4 cups	mashed potatoes
4 x 4-inch circles	puff pastry made with vegetable margarine

Preheat the oven to 350°F. Lightly oil 4 ramekins.

Melt 4 teaspoons of the margarine in a skillet and add the onion, bell pepper, parsnips, savory, garlic, salt, pepper, and veggie mutton; sauté for 4 minutes. Layer the potatoes, followed by veggie mutton mixture, in the ramekins. Place the puff pastry on top and crimp the edges around the ramekin. Brush with the remaining margarine.

Bake for 10–15 minutes, or until pastry golden brown and pie is bubbly.

Great served on a bed of grilled radicchio and mushrooms.

Grilled Radicchio and Mushrooms: Place 1 large, quartered radicchio and ½ cup halved brown mushrooms in a microwave bag with 1 teaspoon water and microwave 5 minutes. Place under broiler and brush with olive oil and balsamic vinegar flavored with 1 teaspoon veggie mint jelly. Once crispy, remove and arrange on serving plates.

shrimp Scampi

Serves 6

2 teaspoons	olive oil
1 pound	linguine pasta
½ cup	vegetable margarine
3 pounds	veggie prawns (about 12–15)
6	garlic cloves, minced
3 teaspoons	chopped fresh tarragon
½ teaspoon	sea salt
1 teaspoon	white pepper
1 cup	organic white wine

Bring a pot of water to a boil, add the olive oil and linguine and cook 10 minutes, or until al dente. Drain and place in cold water for 10 minutes.

Melt the margarine in a skillet, add the veggie prawns, garlic, tarragon, salt, and pepper. Sauté for 3 minutes then add the wine and simmer 3 minutes more.

Meanwhile, drain the linguine and place in colander. Pour boiling water over the pasta to reheat. Place the pasta in a bowl and stir in the "shrimp" mixture. Coat the pasta well and serve immediately.

Serve with garlic bread.

Smoked Veggie Ham
with Melon

Serves 4–6

2 teaspoons	curry powder
½ cup	Quick Orange Marmalade (page 325)
1 cup	vegetable margarine, melted
1	large cantaloupe, wedged and peeled
1 roll	veggie ham, cut into large cubes

Heat a grill or broiler. Mix the curry powder, marmalade, and melted margarine. Add the "ham" cubes to the mixture, basting well. Broil or grill for about 15 minutes. Add cantaloupe wedges during the last 2 minutes.*

Serve over brown rice.

*For variety, place the marinated melon and "ham" on skewers and grill.

Southern Fried "Chicken"

Serves 4

¼ teaspoon	sea salt
1 teaspoon	black pepper
½ teaspoon	red pepper
1 cup	whole-wheat flour
1 cup	corn flakes, crushed
3	garlic cloves, minced
2 tablespoons	minced onion
½ cup	mushroom broth
1 package	veggie chicken nuggets
3 cups	safflower oil for deep-frying

Mix the dry ingredients. Whisk the liquid ingredients and mix into the dry ingredients to form a batter.

Dip the nuggets in the batter and deep-fry until brown and crispy. Serve immediately with your favorite dipping sauce.

Spaghetti Squash Bake

Serves 6

1	medium-large spaghetti squash
4 tablespoons	olive oil
1	medium yellow onion, chopped
6	garlic cloves, minced
1 pound	white mushrooms, sliced
1 pound	veggie crumbles
1 can (12oz)	stewed tomatoes, chopped
1 tablespoon	each chopped fresh basil, oregano, and rosemary
	sea salt and pepper to taste
¼ cup	organic red wine
6 tablespoons	grated veggie parmesan

Cut the squash in half and lay, cut ends down, in a shallow baking dish. Add 8 tablespoons water, cover with saran wrap and cook on high in the microwave for 20 minutes. Allow to cool face up.

Preheat the oven to 375°F. Heat 2 tablespoons of olive oil in a skillet, add onion, garlic, and mushrooms; sauté. Add veggie crumbles and cook until brown. Mix in the stewed tomatoes, herbs, salt, and pepper. Add the wine and simmer for 4 minutes. Using a fork, remove the squash from its shell, being careful not to break the skin. (It will "flake" like strands of spaghetti.) Place the "spaghetti" in a large bowl, add sauce, and blend together.

Fill squash shells with the squash mixture. Top with veggie parmesan and add pepper to taste. Coat an ovenproof baking dish with the remaining olive oil and place the squash in the dish. Bake for about 20 minutes until lightly brown and bubbly.

Serve with garlic bread.

Squash Torta

Serves 12

1 cup	vegan biscuit mix
½ cup	grated veggie parmesan
1 tablespoon	chopped fresh Italian parsley
1 teaspoon	each chopped fresh oregano, basil, and thyme
	salt and pepper
½ cup	olive oil
3	shallots, chopped
	egg replacer for 4 eggs
½	spaghetti squash, cooked and mashed with a fork
2	zucchini, thinly sliced
2	yellow crookneck squash, thinly sliced

Preheat the oven to 350°F.

In a mixing bowl, combine the biscuit mix, cheese, herbs, salt, and pepper. Combine the oil, shallots, and egg replacer in another large bowl. Whisk in the spaghetti squash and combine the mixture with the dry ingredients. Place all the ingredients in 12 x 9 inch baking dish in the following order: quarter of the spaghetti squash and biscuit mix, a layer of zucchini, another quarter of the squash and biscuit mix, a layer of crookneck squash, the rest of the squash and biscuit mix.

Bake for 35 minutes or until brown and set. Cut into slices to serve.

This is great with Savory Gravy (page 320).

Stars and Stripes Timbale

Serves 4

Timbale:

1	very large or 4 medium zucchini, sliced lengthwise
½ cup	stars pasta
1 tablespoon	olive oil
1	onion, thinly sliced
1	red bell pepper, very thinly sliced
2	garlic cloves, minced
3 tablespoons	minced black olives
4 ounces	spinach
¼ cup	shredded veggie mozzarella
	egg replacer for 1 egg
1 tablespoon	oregano
	salt and pepper

Sauce:

4 tablespoons	olive oil
3 tablespoons	organic white wine vinegar
3	garlic cloves, minced
2 tablespoons	fresh oregano
3 cups	stewed tomatoes
1 tablespoon	maple syrup

Blanch the zucchini strips in boiling water for 3 minutes; drain. Oil the bottom and sides of four ramekins; line the dishes with the zucchini, overlapping each dish by 1 inch all round. Boil the pasta for 4 minutes; drain.

Place the olive oil in a skillet, add the onion, bell pepper, and garlic; sauté. Stir in the minced olives and the pasta.

Blanch the spinach, drain, and chop. Mix the cheese, egg replacer, and oregano into the pasta mixture. Season to taste.

Spoon an eighth of the pasta into each ramekin, followed by a layer of spinach; top with another layer of pasta. Fold the zucchini over the pasta and place in an ovenproof baking dish half filled with water. Bake at 350° F for 25 minutes, or until set. To make the sauce, heat the oil in a saucepan, add the garlic, and sauté. Add the remaining sauce ingredients and heat thoroughly. Unmold the ramekins onto a pool of sauce. Shredded daikon radish makes a nice garnish.

Summer "Shrimp" Kabobs

Serves 4

16	veggie shrimp
4	salad cucumbers, trimmed and peeled
½ teaspoon	sea salt
2 bunches	cilantro, stems trimmed off and chopped
1 tablespoon	fresh oregano
1 teaspoon	cumin
½ teaspoon	cinnamon
¼ teaspoon	cloves
½ teaspoon	red-pepper flakes
6	garlic cloves, chopped
½ cup	orange juice
½ cup	lemon juice
1 bunch	red chard, washed, stemmed, and torn into pieces
2 teaspoons	limejuice
¼ cup	olive oil
1 teaspoon	cracked black pepper
4	lemon slices

Slice the cucumbers lengthwise, sprinkle with ½ teaspoon sea salt, and set aside to marinate.

Puree the cilantro, herbs, spices, garlic, and juices in a blender. Marinate the "shrimp" in the cilantro puree for 1 hour. Meanwhile, light the barbecue and allow the coals to fire up. Place the chard in boiling water and blanch for 3–4 minutes. Drain and place in ice water. Drain in colander. Toss with limejuice, oil, and pepper. Place on serving tray or 4 individual plates.

Skewer the "shrimp" and cucumbers. Place over the coals and grill for 1½ minutes each side, basting often. Place the skewers over bed of chard and garnish with lemon slices.

Sushi Delight

Yields 6 large rolls or 36 pieces

Sushi Rice:

2 cups	short-grain rice
2½ cups	water
½ cup	rice vinegar
¼ cup	raw sugar
3 teaspoons	salt

Sushi Rolls:

4 tablespoons	oil
3 tablespoons	sesame seeds
10-ounce package	tofu (cut into strips and marinated in sweet and sour sauce or honey miso sauce overnight)
6 sheets	toasted Sushi Nori
1	avocado, cut into wedges
1	firm cucumber, peeled and cut into strips
1 cup	enoki mushroom
½ cup	daikon radish sprouts

First make the sushi rice. Wash the rice in cold water, then place in a pot. Cover with the water, bring to a boil then reduce heat to low and simmer for 25 minutes. Remove from heat and let stand 10 minutes. (Alternatively, use a rice cooker.)

In a small saucepan, combine the vinegar, sugar, and salt. Heat over a low heat, stirring until the sugar has dissolved. Cool. Place the rice in shallow dish and add the vinegar mixture a little at a time, while fanning the rice with a newspaper. Once the vinegar is dissolved into the rice and the rice is glistening, you're done with the prep. Cover with moist towel to prevent from drying out and leave at room temperature for up to three hours.

To make the sushi rolls, begin by heating the oil and sesame seeds in a skillet. Add the tofu and fry until browned. Remove and drain the tofu on paper towels. Cool. Roll out a bamboo rolling mat or an 8-inch square piece of aluminum foil. Place a sheet of nori on the mat, layer one-sixth of the rice on top. Lay a strip of tofu, avocado, and cucumber over the rice. Follow with the mushrooms and sprouts. Roll up. Repeat until you have used all the ingredients. If you like, cut each roll into six pieces. Serve with tamari, Wasabi Sauce (page 319), and ginger. Eat immediately!

Stuffed Sunburst Stew

Serves 4

¼ cup	olive oil
1	medium yellow onion, diced
4	garlic cloves, minced
1	large tomato, diced
4	sunburst squash, washed, cored, flesh scooped out and reserved
½ cup	vegetable broth
1 teaspoon	cocoa powder
1 teaspoon	maple syrup
	sea salt and pepper to taste

Heat the olive oil in a skillet. Add the onion and garlic; sauté. Add the tomato and reserved squash; sauté then slowly add the vegetable broth. Bring to a boil, reduce the heat, and simmer for 4 minutes. Preheat the oven to 375° F. Rub the squash with oil and salt. Parboil for 5 minutes then place in a baking dish. Add the cocoa and syrup to the sauté mixture and stir well. Remove from the heat. Stuff the squash with the stew and sprinkle with pepper. Bake for 25 minutes.

Tandoori-Style Vegetables

Serves 6, generously

Marinade:

2 cups	plain soy yogurt
2 tablespoons	lemon juice
2 tablespoons	vegetable margarine
2 teaspoons	garam masala
½ teaspoon	chili powder
2	garlic cloves, minced
1 teaspoon	ginger
2 tablespoons	fresh mint
1	jalapeño chili, minced
2 teaspoons	coriander
½ teaspoon	sea salt
1 teaspoon	black pepper
1	small cauliflower, cut into bite-size florets
4	potatoes, cubed
12	cherry tomatoes, red and yellow
6	boiling onions
1	green bell pepper, julienne cut

Combine the marinade ingredients, mixing well. Marinate the veggies in the mixture for at least 30 minutes.

Light the barbecue. Cook the veggies on the grill, basting often with the marinade, until tender and crisp.

This marinade is also great with a veggie chicken. As well as covering the "chicken" with the marinade, make sure you inject it under the "skin" (use one of those culinary needle and syringe kits). Marinate it overnight.

Tempting Tempeh*
Cacciatore

Serves 4

1 pound	smoked tempeh
1 teaspoon	olive oil
1	large white onion, chopped
½ cup	fresh mushrooms
1 teaspoon	chopped fresh parsley
1	bay leaf
½ teaspoon	fresh rosemary
1 teaspoon	fresh basil
½ teaspoon	nutmeg
½ teaspoon	salt
½ teaspoon	black pepper
2	large tomatoes, chopped
4 tablespoons	tomato paste
½ cup	vegetable broth
¼ cup	organic white wine

Slice the tempeh into four portions. Heat the oil in a skillet and brown the onions. Now sauté the mushrooms, and add the herbs, spices, seasoning, tomatoes, tomato paste, and broth. Bring the sauce to a boil then add the wine to deglaze the sauce. Add the tempeh and simmer for 20 minutes. Serve over pasta.

* You can substitute tofu or veggie chicken for the tempeh.

Tempura

Serves 12

Batter:

1¼ cups	ice water
1 tablespoon	tamari
1 cup	flour
½ teaspoon	sea salt
¼ teaspoon	baking soda

Sauce:

⅔ cup	tamari
3 tablespoons	rice wine
2 tablespoons	grated ginger root
1 tablespoon	cane sugar

mushrooms
eggplant
asparagus tips
potatoes
sweet potatoes
broccoli florets
veggie shrimp or veggie fish

Mix the batter ingredients together using a whisk just before you are ready to cook. Dip and coat your choice of veggies and "seafood." Fry the tempura in safflower oil then drain on paper towels. Mix the ingredients for the dipping sauce and heat gently. Serve the tempura with the warm dipping sauce.

Tofu... Jerked

Serves 4

Marinade:

1 cup	mango, papaya, or apple juice
4 tablespoons	grated onion
4 tablespoons	minced garlic
2 tablespoons	tamari
3 tablespoons	red pepper
3 tablespoons	white wine vinegar
1 tablespoon	safflower oil
1 tablespoon	grated ginger root
2 teaspoons	allspice
½ teaspoon	cinnamon
1 teaspoon	nutmeg
1 teaspoon	black pepper
½ teaspoon	thyme
10 ounces	firm tofu, cubed
1 bunch	scallions, minced
1 teaspoon	cornstarch

Process all the marinade ingredients. Marinate the tofu and scallions in the sauce for 24 hours.

Broil or barbeque the tofu. Thicken the marinade with the cornstarch, heat, and pour the sauce over the tofu. Serve over brown rice.

Tomato Phyllo Pie

Serves 12

2 tablespoons	olive oil
1½ cups	vegetable margarine
1	medium white onion, thinly sliced
2 teaspoons	fresh thyme
1 teaspoon	fresh oregano
2 teaspoons	sea salt
1 teaspoon	pepper
1 package	phyllo pastry
2 cups	veggie mozzarella, shredded
12	large roma tomatoes, sliced
½ cup	grated veggie romano or parmesan

Preheat the oven to 375°F.

Lightly oil a large shallow ovenproof baking dish with the olive oil.

Melt the margarine in a skillet, add the onions, herbs, salt, and pepper; sauté.

Unwrap the pastry and place one sheet on the bottom of the oiled dish. Spread some of the margarine and onion mixture over it, followed by some shredded veggie mozzarella. Repeat these three layers until the dish is nearly full then top it with a layer with tomato slices followed by onion mixture and the romano or parmesan. Bake for 20 minutes.

Tom's Stuffed Spuds

Serves 2

2	extra large russet baking potatoes
4 tablespoons	vegetable margarine
1	leek, trimmed and sliced
2	carrots, sliced
2	parsnips, sliced
1 cup	white mushrooms, sliced
2 cups	spinach, chopped
3 tablespoons	sesame oil
2 teaspoons	black pepper
4 tablespoons	tamari
1 quantity	Savory Gravy or World's Best Gravy recipe (pages 320 and 321)

Preheat the oven to 450°F.

Scrub the potatoes and bake until tender, about 50 minutes.

In a skillet, stir-fry the leek, carrot, parsnips, mushroom, and spinach in sesame oil, pepper, and tamari. When the potatoes are ready, cut in two, scoop out the flesh into a bowl, and mash. Rub the potato skins with margarine. Fold the veggies into the mashed potato and season to taste with salt and pepper. Stuff the potato skins with the mixture, return to the oven and bake 7–10 minutes until slightly browned and the top is crispy. Top with your choice of gravy. Be hungry ... be very hungry!

Too-Foo Yung

Serves 6

Patties:

1 teaspoon	grated ginger root
½ cup	fresh chopped green beans
1	large carrot, grated
½ cup	water chestnuts, chopped
2	scallions, chopped
½ cup	bean sprouts
10 ounces	firm tofu
½ teaspoon	sea salt
¼ teaspoon	black pepper
	safflower oil for frying

Sauce:

1 cup	vegetable broth
1 tablespoon	arrowroot
1 tablespoon	tamari
1 tablespoon	minced garlic
1 tablespoon	sugar

Process the patty ingredients. Heat the oil in a skillet and pour in 4 tablespoons of patty batter; fry 5 minutes on each side. Repeat until all the batter is used. Meanwhile, mix together the sauce ingredients and heat in a saucepan to thicken.

Fold each patty over once and serve with the sauce.

Vegan Cordon Bleu

Serves 2

1 package	veggie chicken breasts
4 tablespoons	olive oil
1	garlic clove, minced
1 handful	fresh basil, chopped
½ cup	broccoli florets, parboiled
4 slices	veggie mozzarella cheese
1 cup	organic white wine
¼ cup	slivered almonds

Cut the "breasts" in half and then slice again, lengthwise.

Heat the oil in a skillet with the garlic and basil, add the "breasts" and sear for about 4 minutes. Remove from the heat. Stuff the "breasts" with broccoli and wrap veggie slices securely around each one.

Add wine to the pan and deglaze over high heat. Top the "breasts" with the almonds and serve with the sauce.

Vegan Mole

Serves 6

½ cup	raw pumpkin seeds
1 teaspoon	cumin seed
½ teaspoon	pepper
¼ teaspoon	fresh thyme
¼ teaspoon	fresh oregano
8	tomatillos, husked and quartered
1	jalapeño chili, stemmed and seeded
2	romaine lettuce leaves
1	white onion, sliced
2	garlic cloves
1 bunch	cilantro
¼ teaspoon	cinnamon
1 teaspoon	sea salt
2 tablespoon	olive oil
2 cups	vegetable broth
4	veggie chicken breasts, cut in half or 2 packages veggie chicken nuggets
1	raw parsnip, sliced paper thin

Preheat oven to 350° F. In a skillet, toast the pumpkin seeds, cumin seeds, pepper, thyme, and oregano over low heat for 5 minutes. Cool. Grind up and reserve.

Mix the tomatillos, chili, romaine, onion, garlic, cilantro, cinnamon, and salt. Puree in a blender until smooth. Heat the olive oil in a skillet. Add the puree, allow it to sizzle for about 30 seconds then add the vegetable broth. Reduce the heat and simmer 10 minutes. After 10 minutes turn up the heat and boil; stir in the ground up seed mixture. Remove from the heat after 1 minute. Puree and place mole in an ovenproof baking dish. Add the "chicken," cover with foil, and bake 20 minutes. Garnish with parsnips and serve over brown rice or with steamed corn tortillas.

Vegabalaya

Serves 4–6

1	large red onion, chopped
4	garlic cloves, minced
1	red bell pepper, chopped
1	large carrot, sliced
2	bay leaves
½ pound	veggie sausage, sliced
½ pound	veggie chicken, chopped
6	celery ribs, chopped
1 teaspoon	white pepper
1 teaspoon	cayenne pepper
1 teaspoon	black pepper
1 teaspoon	Cajun spice
2 cups	stewed tomatoes
3 cups	okra, sliced
1 cup	artichoke hearts, chopped
2 cups	rice
3 cups	vegetable broth
12	veggie shrimp
12	asparagus spears, sliced
	lemon wedges

Heat 2–3 tablespoons of oil in a skillet and sauté the onions until beginning to soften. Add the garlic, red peppers, carrot, bay leaves, and sausage and cook 5 minutes, or until the sausage is browned. Add the "chicken," celery, the various dry peppers and spices and continue to cook until the chicken is browned. Add the tomatoes, okra, artichokes, and rice; reduce the heat to medium and simmer 7–10 minutes, stirring often. Add the vegetable broth and continue to cook an additional 10 minutes. Add more broth by the tablespoon as needed. Place the veggie shrimp and asparagus spears on top of the rice and steam until al dente. Garnish with a sprinkle of Cajun spice and lemon wedges.

Vegacotti

Serves 8

1 package	manicotti pasta
2 teaspoons	olive oil
½	yellow onion, chopped
6	garlic cloves, minced
1 pound	porcini mushrooms, sliced
½ teaspoon	each fresh oregano, rosemary, basil, and tarragon
½ teaspoon	sea salt
½ teaspoon	white pepper
8	Italian tomatoes, chopped
1 can	black olives, crumbled
1 cup	steamed mixed vegetables
8-ounce package	shredded veggie mozzarella
6 tablespoons	grated veggie parmesan
¼ cup	veggie sour cream

Cook the pasta in boiling water for 10 minutes. Cool in cold water for 10 minutes, drain, and pat dry.

Heat the olive oil in a pan and add the onion, garlic, porcini, herbs, salt, and pepper; sauté. Reserve ¼ cup of the tomatoes and add the rest to the pan, along with the olives and vegetables; simmer 7 minutes. Allow to cool for 10 minutes.

Reserve ⅛ cup of the shredded "mozzarella" and a tablespoon of the "parmesan" and mix the remainder into the cooled mixture along with the veggie cream. Stuff the pasta with the mixture. Place the reserved tomatoes in the bottom of an ovenproof dish and sprinkle over 4 drops of olive oil. Nest the vegacotti in the dish and sprinkle with the remaining veggie cheeses. Bake at 375° F until bubbly, about 10–15 minutes.

Vegetable Fajitas with Sizzling Chili Lime Sauce

Serves 4

2	medium zucchinis
2	yellow squash
4	plum tomatoes
4	scallions

Marinade:

½ cup	safflower oil
Juice of 1	lime
2	garlic cloves, chopped
½ teaspoon	sea salt
1 teaspoon	chili powder
½ teaspoon	cumin
8	wheat tortillas
	veggie cheese shreds or veggie sour cream to serve

Light a grill or barbecue. Cut the vegetables into wedges or strips. Combine the marinade ingredients and toss with the vegetables. Marinate up to 1 hour. Grill or cook the vegetables until hot, juicy, and sizzling, 6–10 minutes. Serve with warm wheat tortillas and veggie cheese shreds or veggie sour cream.

Vegetable Turnovers

Serves 4

3 tablespoons	vegetable margarine
¼ cup	sliced mushrooms
3 teaspoons	chopped onion
3	garlic cloves, minced
¼ cup	mixed peas, corn, green beans, broccoli (diced)
2 teaspoons	diced green bell pepper
½ teaspoon	chopped fresh sage
2 teaspoons	chopped fresh parsley
	salt and pepper to taste
½ cup	veggie mozzarella shreds
1 package	phyllo dough, thawed, unfolded, and cut into quarters

Preheat oven to 400° F.

Melt the margarine in a skillet, add the mushrooms, onion, and garlic; sauté. Add the rest of the veggies, then the herbs, and season with salt and pepper. Fold in the shreds. Divide the mixture into 4 portions. Place each portion on layered sheets of dough and fold over. If you like, brush the pastry with oat milk, then crimp the edges with a fork. Place on a cookie sheet and bake for 30 minutes.

Serve with a side of Savory Gravy (see page 320).

Veggie Lamb and Snow Pea Stir-Fry

Serves 2

3 tablespoons	sesame oil
8 ounces	veggie lamb
1 teaspoon	grated ginger root
1 teaspoon	white pepper
1 pound	snow peas, washed and trimmed
3 tablespoons	tamari
1 cup	sliced water chestnuts
2 cups	almond milk
2 tablespoons	cornstarch

Heat the oil in skillet, add the "lamb" and seasonings and stir-fry over a high heat for 2 minutes. Add the snow peas and tamari; cook 3 minutes more. Reduce heat, add the chestnuts, and slowly add the almond milk. Simmer for 4 minutes.

Remove ¼ cup liquid from the pan and allow it to cool. Mix the cornstarch with the liquid and slowly reintroduce it to the pan. Allow the sauce to thicken 1 minute more.

Serve with brown rice.

Veggie Lobster Tarra-gone!

Serves 4

2	limes
1	veggie lobster, thawed
4 tablespoons	fresh tarragon
	salt and black pepper to taste
4 tablespoons	vegetable margarine
1 cup	bread crumbs
1 cup	organic Chardonnay

Preheat the oven to 375° F.

Peel the limes and break into wedges. Make four 1-inch cuts diagonally into the "lobster" and stuff with the tarragon. Sprinkle to taste with salt and pepper.

Combine the margarine and bread crumbs, pat the mixture over the lobster, and place in an ovenproof dish. Squeeze some lime over the "lobster" and arrange the remaining slices around it. Pour on the wine. Bake until the bread crumbs are lightly browned and crispy, about 15–20 minutes.

Great with Pacifica Dressing (page 304) and a baked potato.

Veggie Scallops and Soba

Serves 6

Veggie Scallops:

½ cup	tamari
½ cup	lemon juice
2 teaspoons	grated ginger root
1 tablespoon	five-spice seasoning
1 tablespoon	cane syrup
2 tablespoons	sesame oil
30	veggie scallops

Soba:

6 ounces	buckwheat noodles
1 teaspoon	sesame oil
1	yellow bell pepper, julienne cut
1	cucumber, julienne cut
½	red onion, julienne cut
1 tablespoon	rice vinegar
¼ teaspoon	sea salt

First marinate the scallops. Whisk together the tamari, lemon juice, ginger root, seasoning, syrup, and oil. Marinate the veggie scallops overnight in the mixture. In a hot skillet, sauté the scallops 6 minutes, allowing them to blacken slightly. Remove the scallops from the pan and reserve. Pour the marinade into the pan and bring to a boil over medium heat. Now lower the heat and add the scallops; heat for 2 minutes to reduce.

Meanwhile make the soba. Place the noodles and 1 cup of cold water in boiling water. Allow it to boil then add another cup of cold water; boil, remove from heat, and drain. Toss the noodles with sesame oil. Toss the remaining ingredients together then mix with the noodles. Serve the scallops over the noodles and top with the reduced marinade.

Veggie Soft Tacos

Serves 4 generously, party style!

1 cup	vegan soy hamburger
½ teaspoon	cumin
½ teaspoon	pepper
1 cup	canned black beans
1 cup	thinly sliced scallions
1 cup	diced tomatoes
1 cup	chopped black olives
1 cup	shredded red-leaf lettuce
1 cup	cilantro, chopped
1 cup	shredded veggie cheddar cheese
1 cup	jalapeño chilies, diced
1 cup	tomatillo salsa
1 cup	guacamole
12	small corn tortillas
	your favorite condiments...

Brown the vegan soy hamburger in a skillet, mixing in the cumin and pepper.

Heat the black beans for 3 minutes in the microwave.

Place moistened paper towels between the tortillas. Place them in a tortilla warmer and heat in the microwave for 3 minutes.

Arrange the fillings and condiments in dishes, or a lazy Susan, so that guests can help themselves.

Veggie Tofu Terrine

Serves 8

2 tablespoons	olive oil
1 cup	shallots, minced
1 cup	minced garlic
1 bunch	thyme, chopped
3 sprigs	rosemary, chopped
2 cups	beet juice
¼ cup	red wine vinegar
7 tablespoons	agar agar
1 block	firm tofu, cut into 8 slices
8	dry-packed sun-dried tomatoes
16	baby carrots, steamed and sliced
½ bunch	basil, sliced

Heat the oil in a skillet, add the shallots and garlic; sauté. Add the thyme, rosemary, and beet juice and bring to a boil. Reduce to a simmer; add vinegar and agar agar. Cook 2 minutes.

In an ovenproof dish layer the tofu, tomato, carrot, basil, and beet sauce. Place the dish within larger pan of water and bake in the oven at 300° F for 50 minutes, or until set. Serve with Italian bread.

Vintage Street Veggie Loaf

Serves 8

1 pound	vegan soy hamburger
½ cup	chopped onion
¼ cup	sliced mushrooms
1	garlic clove, minced
2 tablespoons	tamari
1 cup	brown rice
½ cup	rolled oats
½ cup	almond milk
½ tablespoon	chopped fresh sage
¼ teaspoon	black pepper
6 ounces	plain soy yogurt

Preheat the oven to 350° F.

Combine all the ingredients in a large bowl. Form into a loaf and place in an oiled bread pan. Bake for 45–60 minutes.

Serve with World's Best Veggie Gravy and Veg-up, (pages 321 and 319). Leftovers make a great sandwich filling!

Zoran's "Pork Meatballs" in Green Sauce

Serves 4–6

"Pork Meatballs":

10½ ounces	diced vegetable pork
¼ cup	garlic-seasoned breadcrumbs
½ cup	black beans, cooked
2 ounces	soy cream cheese
5	garlic cloves, minced
2 tablespoons	minced red onion
½ cup	vegetable broth
Dash of	red pepper
	flour
	safflower oil

Green Sauce:

2 tablespoons	olive oil
2 tablespoons	minced shallot
4	garlic cloves, minced
4 teaspoons	flour
¼ cup	organic white wine
½ cup	vegetable broth
2 tablespoons	multigrain milk
½ cup	minced parsley
	salt and pepper to taste

Combine all the "meatball" ingredients, except the flour and oil, and form into balls.

Roll the balls in flour and fry in oil for 3 minutes. Remove and drain on paper towels.

Alternatively, the "meatballs" can be baked at 350° F for 10 minutes, or until browned.

Heat the oil for the sauce, add the shallot and garlic; sauté. Add the flour and then blend in the wine, broth, milk, parsley, and seasoning. Stir constantly, allowing it to thicken. Add the "meatballs," coat completely and heat thoroughly. Serve as a fondue or main course.

Companion Pleasures:

VEGGIES, BEANS AND GRAINS...

TO COMPLEMENT ENTREES OR

TO BE SERVED A LA CARTE

Bar-B-Q Leeks in Horseradish Sauce

Serves 4

12	medium leeks, washed well, trimmed, and halved lengthwise
2 tablespoons	olive oil
1 teaspoon	sea salt
½ teaspoon	cracked black pepper
½ cup	veggie sour cream
1 tablespoon	horseradish paste
3 teaspoons	pickled ginger root

Light the barbecue and allow the coals to heat up. Place the leeks on aluminum foil and brush with oil, salt, and pepper. Seal the foil and cook over the coals under tender, about 35–40 minutes.

Combine the sour cream, horseradish, and ginger. Spoon over the leeks and serve.

Basil Veggie Balls

Serves 6

1	eggplant, halved
2	yellow crookneck squash
2	zucchini
6	boiling onions
1 bunch	basil
¼ cup	vegetable margarine, melted
6	cherry tomatoes
¼ cup	veggie parmesan
	sea salt and pepper

Use a melon baller to carve balls from the center of the eggplant halves, the crookneck, and the zucchini.

Place the eggplant, squashes and zucchini balls, and onions in a double boiler or steamer. Add the margarine and basil. Steam until tender. Add the tomatoes, veggie parmesan, and seasoning to taste; mix well. Place the mixture in the eggplant shells. Bake for 10 minutes at 350°F.

Blow Me Down! Lemon Spinach

Serves 4

2 bunches	spinach, very well washed and chopped
1 tablespoon	sea salt
3 tablespoons	olive oil
3	garlic cloves, minced
Juice of 2	lemons

Place the spinach, sea salt, and 3 cups of water in a saucepan; boil for 8 minutes then drain. Heat the oil in a skillet, add the garlic and spinach; cook for 2 minutes. Add the lemon juice and serve immediately.

Broccoli Croissants

Serves 12

2 cups	broccoli florets, chopped
1 tablespoon	chopped onion
1 cup	white mushrooms, sliced
¼ teaspoon	fresh sage
¼ teaspoon	fresh thyme
1 teaspoon	sea salt
½ teaspoon	white pepper
Juice of 1	lemon
½ cup	bread crumbs
½ cup	multigrain milk
¼ cup	veggie cheddar shreds
1 quantity	Quick-Rise Bread Dough recipe (page 385)
12 teaspoons	vegetable margarine, melted
2	garlic cloves, minced

Parboil the broccoli with the onions and mushrooms for 4 minutes. Drain well.

Mix the seasonings with the crumbs and milk. Add the vegetables and fold in the veggie cheese.

Preheat the oven to 425° F. Roll out the dough and cut into 12 triangles.

Mix the margarine and garlic in a dish. Spoon 2–3 teaspoons of vegetable filling onto the dough triangles and roll to form croissants. Place the croissants, seam side down, on an oiled cookie sheet. Baste with the margarine and bake for 8 minutes or until browned.

Broiled Tomatoes

Serves 8

4 tablespoons	vegetable margarine
4	large tomatoes, cut in half
4 tablespoons	diced onion
4 tablespoons	chopped fresh dill
½ cup	vegan mayonnaise dressing

Preheat the oven to 325°F.

Spread the margarine on the tomato halves; broil 6 minutes or until warm and juicy. Cook the onions in the microwave 2 minutes. Mix the dill and vegan mayonnaise dressing with the onion and dollop onto the warm tomatoes.

Brussels Sprout Slaw

Serves 8

4 tablespoons	vegetable margarine
2 tablespoons	fresh thyme
4 tablespoons	pine nuts
2 pounds	brussels sprouts, washed and thinly sliced
2	granny smith apples, peeled, cored, and shredded
	salt and pepper

Heat the vegetable margarine in a skillet. Add the thyme and pine nuts; brown. Add the Brussels sprouts and flash cook for about 6 minutes. Slowly add the apples and continue to simmer 4 minutes longer. Season to taste with salt and pepper. Serve warm.

Cajun Black Bean Cakes

Serves 4

¾ cup	black beans
6 cups	vegetable broth
2	carrots, finely chopped
1	celery rib, finely chopped
1	jalapeño chili, roasted, peeled, seeded, and diced
½ cup	chopped cilantro
1 tablespoon	chili powder
1 tablespoon	cumin
	sea salt and pepper to taste
	olive oil for frying

Soak the beans overnight. Rinse several times until the water becomes clear.

Place the beans and vegetable broth in soup pot, add the carrots and celery, and cook for 1½ hours, or until tender. Drain. Puree to make about 3 cups. Mix in the remaining ingredients, except the olive oil.

Divide the bean mixture into four and place each piece between wax paper, pressing to form patties. Heat the oil in a skillet, add the patties and fry on each side until browned and crispy.

Great served with veggie sour cream, red salsa, and additional sautéed chilies and bell peppers.

Chickpeas in Saffron

Serves 6

1 pound	chickpeas
3 tablespoons	olive oil
3	tomatoes, chopped
	sea salt and black pepper to taste
1 tablespoon	red pepper
½ teaspoon	saffron or 2 threads

Place the chickpeas in a pot, cover with water, and cook for 1½ hours. Reserve ½ cup of the liquid.

Place the olive oil, tomato, salt, and pepper in a saucepan; sauté. Mix all the ingredients together, except the saffron, and simmer for 30 minutes. Add the saffron to the pan and cook for 3 minutes.

Couscous Pockets

Serves 4

2 sheets	phyllo dough
4 tablespoons	vegetable margarine, melted
2 teaspoons	chopped fresh parsley
1	scallion, thinly sliced
	olive oil
1 cup	couscous, cooked
¼ cup	diced olives
	sea salt
	balsamic vinegar

Preheat the oven to 325°F.

Lay out the pastry, brush with the melted margarine and sprinkle with parsley. Cut into 4-inch squares. Layer three pieces, brushing each layer with margarine and sprinkling with parsley.

Sauté the scallion in 1 teaspoon of olive oil. Mix the scallion with the cooked couscous and the olives, and add salt to taste.

Place 2 tablespoons of the couscous mixture on each square of dough and wrap, twisting the top. Bake for 5 minutes, or until browned. Reduce some balsamic vinegar in a pan to intensify the flavor. Brush over the pockets before serving.

Serve with Exotic Grilled Vegetables (page 125).

Dilled Brussels Sprouts

Serves 4

1 pound	brussels sprouts, washed
4 tablespoons	water
2 tablespoons	lemon juice
1 tablespoon	chopped fresh dill weed
4 tablespoons	vegetable margarine

Remove any yellow outer leaves from the sprouts, cut the bottom of the stem off, and make a cross in the bottom using the point of a small sharp knife. Place all the ingredients, except the margarine, in large freezer bag and microwave 10 minutes. Drain, place in a serving bowl, and add the margarine.

Fennel in Almond Sauce

Serves 6

¼ cup	vegetable margarine
1	large fennel bulb, trimmed and cut into 1-inch pieces
1 tablespoon	sea salt
½ teaspoon	white pepper
1 tablespoon	chopped fresh chives
2 tablespoons	chopped red onion
1 cup	almond milk
½ cup	vegetable broth
1 tablespoon	rye flour
1 cup	slivered almonds, toasted

Melt the margarine in a saucepan, add the fennel, salt, and pepper; simmer for 10 minutes.

Add the chives and onions and simmer for a further 10 minutes. Add the almond milk and ¼ cup of the vegetable broth and bring to a boil.

Mix the remaining cold broth with the flour. Add a dash of salt and mix well. Turn into the saucepan and cook for 2 minutes to allow the sauce to thicken. Add the almonds and serve.

Festive Acorn Rings

Serves 8

2 tablespoons	safflower oil
1 cup	vegetable margarine, melted
2 teaspoons	sea salt
2 teaspoons	cinnamon
¼ cup	hickory syrup
2	acorn squash, seeded and sliced into rings
¼ cup	grated veggie parmesan

Preheat the oven to 350° F.

Line a cookie sheet with foil and lightly brush with
2 tablespoons of safflower oil. Combine the margarine, salt,
cinnamon, and syrup. Mix well. Dip the acorn rings in the
mixture. Sprinkle with "cheese" and place on the cookie sheet.
Bake for about 30 minutes until crispy brown, turning once.

Fried Green Tomatoes 2004

Serves 8

4 cups	crushed cornflake cereal
¼ teaspoon	sea salt
½ teaspoon	black pepper
1 teaspoon	celery seed
	egg replacer for 1 egg
1 cup	multigrain milk
4	large green tomatoes, washed, cored, and sliced

Combine the cereal, salt, pepper, and celery seed. Mix the egg replacer with the milk. Dip the tomatoes in milk and then in the cereal mixture. Fry in oil and drain well.

Serve with Ranch Dressing (page 305).

Garlic Custard

Serves 6

6 heads of	garlic, roasted, peeled, and mashed
¼ cup	veggie mozzarella, shredded
¼ cup	bread crumbs
½ cup	soft tofu
2 cups	almond milk
½ teaspoon	sea salt
½ teaspoon	pepper
2 tablespoons	sun-dried tomatoes in oil
	fresh parsley to garnish

Preheat the oven to 350°F.

Whisk together all the ingredients, except the tomatoes, and place on a medium heat until the mixture thickens, the garlic softens, and it comes to a boil. Divide the mixture between 6 oiled ramekins. Bake for 50 minutes. Allow to cool for 10 minutes then invert. Garnish the top with tomatoes and parsley.

Serve with veggie pepper steak or veggie chicken.

Garlic Roasted Potatoes

Serves 12

10	red potatoes, washed and quartered
1 head of	garlic, broken down into cloves and chopped
1 large bunch	Italian parsley, chopped
Juice of 1	lemon
¼ cup	olive oil

Place all the ingredients in a bowl and mix. Line a cookie sheet with aluminum foil and spread the vegetables on the sheet. Cook at 425° F until done, about 45 minutes or so.

This dish is also good for barbecues. Place all the ingredients in bowl and mix. Wrap in aluminum foil, place on top of hot coals, and cook 45 minutes, or until done. Unwrap for the last 5 minutes to allow the potato skins to brown. You can wrap the potatoes in individual packets and serve one per person.

Glazed Turnips

Serves 6

10	small turnips, peeled and diced
1½ cups	vegetable broth
4 tablespoons	vegetable margarine
2 tablespoons	hickory shagbark syrup
½ teaspoon	sea salt
2 tablespoons	chopped fresh parsley

Place all the ingredients, except the parsley, in a skillet. Bring to a boil then reduce the heat and simmer for about 20 minutes until the liquid has thickened and the turnips are tender.

Sprinkle with parsley.

Gourmet Rings

Serves 4

1 teaspoon	red pepper
1 teaspoon	cumin
1 teaspoon	coriander
1 teaspoon	sea salt
¼ cup	crushed wheat flakes
½ cup	wheat flour
1 cup	vegetable broth
2	large white onions, cut into thick slices
2	large red onions, cut into thick slices
6 cups	olive oil

Mix the seasonings, wheat flakes, and flour together. Add the vegetable broth to make a paste. Dip the onions in the paste and deep-fry them in the hot oil until browned and crispy. Drain well before serving.

Green Bean Medley

Serves 4–6

3 tablespoons	olive oil
1 pound	green beans, trimmed and washed
1	red bell pepper, cut into strips
1	medium white onion, thinly sliced
¼ cup	sliced almonds
1 teaspoon	fresh thyme

Heat the oil in a skillet, add the remaining ingredients, and sauté until the beans are softened to your liking. Serve immediately.

Hickory Baked Yams

Serves 6

2	large yams, washed
¼ cup	limejuice
4 tablespoons	lemon juice
3 tablespoons	vegetable margarine
½ cup	hickory shagbark syrup
1 teaspoon	sea salt
½ teaspoon	black pepper
½ cup	veggie sour cream

Preheat the oven to 325° F.

Peel the yams, place in an oiled ovenproof dish, and sprinkle with limejuice. Bake for 50 minutes, or until done.

Mash the yams, adding the lemon juice, margarine, syrup, salt, and pepper. Place in a baking dish and return to the oven for 15 minutes. Remove from the oven and garnish with sour cream.

"Mac and Cheese"

Serves 8

2 tablespoons	olive oil
1 pound	elbow macaroni
1 teaspoon	powdered vegetable seasoning
1 teaspoon	pepper
3 tablespoons	tamari
6 tablespoons	vegetable margarine
6 slices	each of veggie cheddar, mozzarella, and Swiss cheese
1 cup	multigrain milk
3 tablespoons	grated veggie parmesan

Add the olive oil to a large pan of boiling water, add the pasta, and cook according to package directions. Once done, drain and season with vegetable seasoning, pepper, and tamari. Return to a low heat. Add the margarine and 6 veggie mozzarella slices. Allow this to melt into the mixture as you slowly add the multigrain milk. Remove from heat.

Place a layer of the macaroni mixture in an ovenproof dish. Top this with a layer of veggie cheese, alternating the cheddar and Swiss cheese slices with the pasta until the dish is filled. Sprinkle the veggie parmesan over the top layer.

Bake at 375°F for 35 minutes, or until bubbly. Let stand 5 minutes before serving. For a variation, mix ¾ cup bread crumbs, 4 teaspoons vegetable margarine, and ½ teaspoon pepper with the grated veggie parmesan.

Mushroom Fettuccine Casserole

Serves 12

3 tablespoons	olive oil
2 pounds	fettuccine pasta
½ cup	vegetable margarine
1 pound	oyster mushrooms, whole
1 pound	white mushrooms, sliced
3	garlic cloves, minced
1 cup	organic white wine
1 cup	multigrain milk
2 teaspoons	tamari
Dash of	sea salt
1 teaspoon	black pepper
1 cup	soy cream cheese
1¼ cups	veggie mozzarella, shredded
3 tablespoons	cornstarch mixed with ½ cup multigrain milk
¾ cup	grated veggie romano cheese
1½ cups	bread crumbs

Add the olive oil to a large pan of boiling water, add the pasta, and cook according to package directions. Drain and rinse in cold water.

Preheat the oven to 350°F. Melt the margarine in a saucepan, add the mushrooms and garlic, and sauté over medium heat for 4 minutes. Deglaze with the wine. Add the milk, seasonings, soy cream cheese, and veggie mozzarella; simmer until the cheese has melted. Stir in the cornstarch mixture. In a large mixing bowl, combine the fettuccine and white sauce. Coat the pasta well. Mix the romano and bread crumbs together. Place the pasta mixture in an ovenproof baking dish and top with the breadcrumb mixture. Bake for 30–40 minutes until bubbly and lightly browned.

New Year's Black-Eyed Peas

Serves 12

2 cups	black-eyed peas
8 cups	vegetable broth
1	yellow onion, chopped
2 teaspoons	sea salt
1 tablespoon	red-pepper flakes
1 cup	brown rice
½ cup	chopped veggie ham
12	tomatoes
1 bunch	parsley, chopped

Soak the peas in water overnight then rinse well. Place the peas, broth, onion, salt, and pepper flakes in a large pot and bring to a boil. Reduce the heat and add the rice, veggie ham, and tomatoes. Cover and cook for 1 hour. Add the parsley and cook 20 minutes more.

Old-World Roasted Sweet Potatoes

Serves 6

1 teaspoon	coriander
½ teaspoon	fennel seeds
½ teaspoon	oregano
1 teaspoon	sea salt
½ teaspoon	black pepper
2 pounds	medium sweet potatoes, scrubbed and sliced into 1-inch wedges
4 tablespoons	olive oil

Place all the spices in bowl, add the potato wedges, and toss. Place the oil on a cookie sheet, add the wedges, and toss them to coat with the oil.

Bake at 425°F until golden, about 20 minutes.

Pepper-Fried Corn

Serves 4

4 ears	of white corn
3 tablespoons	water
½ teaspoon	sea salt
2 tablespoons	black pepper
1 tablespoon	red-pepper flakes
6 tablespoons	olive oil

Remove husks from the corn, wash, and place in a large freezer bag with the water and salt. Microwave 8 minutes. Cut the corn from the cob. Heat the oil in a skillet, add the corn and pepper; sear 2–3 minutes. Remove from the heat and serve.

Red Okra Polenta

Serves 4

2 cups	tomato juice
½ pound	okra
1 teaspoon	sea salt
1 cup	yellow cornmeal
2 tablespoons	vegetable margarine
1	medium tomato, cut into slices
4 tablespoons	chopped fresh parsley

Place the tomato juice, okra, and salt in a saucepan and bring to a boil. Reduce the heat, cover, and simmer for 10 minutes. Pour in the cornmeal, stirring constantly. Cook on medium heat until thickened, about 5 minutes. Allow the mixture to cool then form into cakes. Spread with the margarine and garnish with a tomato slice and parsley.

Rotonda Onion Cups

Serves 4

4	medium boiling onions, boiled
4 sprigs	rosemary
4 teaspoons	vegetable margarine
¼ cup	shredded veggie romano and parmesan
½ teaspoon	sea salt
1 teaspoon	pepper
1 cup	bread crumbs
1	medium tomato, sliced
½ teaspoon	celery seed

Preheat the oven to 325°F.

Core the onions. Spear each onion with a sprig of rosemary.

Finely chop the centers and sauté in 3 teaspoons of margarine. Mix with the salt, pepper, cheeses, and bread crumbs. Fill the onions with the mixture, top with tomato slice and sprinkle with celery seed. Brush with the remaining margarine. Bake 8–10 minutes, or until cheeses are melted and tomato "cap" is browned.

Scalloped Rutabagas

Serves 6

2 pounds	rutabagas, peeled and sliced
1 bunch	Italian parsley
2 tablespoons	vegetable margarine
1	jalapeño pepper
2	shallots, thinly sliced
1	garlic clove, minced
½ cup	vegetable broth
1 cup	multigrain milk
	sea salt and pepper
¼ cup	grated veggie parmesan

Cook the rutabagas in salted, boiling water for 5 minutes; remove and pat dry. Cook parsley in the same water for 5 minutes; drain.

Melt the margarine in a skillet, add the pepper, shallots, and garlic and sauté for 10 minutes. Add the broth and cook until reduced in half. Add the milk and simmer 8 minutes, again reducing the sauce. Stir in the parsley, season with salt and pepper, and cook for about 4 minutes to thicken.

Preheat the oven to 400° F. Grease a 6- x 12-inch baking dish. Arrange half the rutabagas in dish and season with salt and pepper. Layer half the parsley sauce over the rutabagas and repeat the layers. Sprinkle the veggie parmesan cheese over the final layer, then cover with aluminum foil and bake for 50 minutes or until bubbly.

Smashed Potatoes

Serves 10

5 pounds	russet potatoes, washed, scrubbed (not peeled), and quartered
1½ cups	multigrain milk
½ cup	vegetable margarine
5	garlic cloves, minced
	sea salt and pepper to taste

Place the potatoes in a pan of water, cook until boiling then reduce heat and simmer until done. Drain well. Add the remaining ingredients and whip with a beater.

Thai Carrots

Serves 4–6

1 pound	baby carrots
1 tablespoon	olive oil
1 tablespoon	arrowroot
3 tablespoons	cider vinegar
2 tablespoons	maple syrup
¼ cup	tomato paste
1 tablespoon	tamari
1	bell pepper, sliced
1	chili pepper, seeded and peeled
	salt and pepper to taste

Bring a pan of water to a boil. Add the carrots and cook 8 minutes. Transfer to preheated skillet, add the oil and fry 5 minutes. Combine the remaining ingredients and add to the carrots. Simmer for 5 minutes.

Whammy Banammy Yams

Serves 6

4	large yams
4 tablespoons	vegetable margarine
1 cup	almond milk
2 teaspoons	cinnamon
2	bananas, pureed

Preheat the oven to 350° F.

Peel and boil the yams. Once tender, drain. Add the margarine, milk, and cinnamon. Whip together then add the pureed bananas. Pour into greased ramekins and bake for 20 minutes, or until browned.

Break-Out-the-Breath-Mints
Wisconsin Onions

Serves 6

1 pound	boiling onions, peeled
1 teaspoon	sea salt
¼ cup	oat milk
½ cup	veggie sour cream
8 ounces	veggie cheddar, shredded
2 teaspoons	tamari
1 teaspoon	white pepper
2 tablespoons	chopped fresh tarragon

Place the onions and salt in a pan, cover with water, and bring to a boil. Simmer until tender, 8 minutes or so. Drain.

In a saucepan, whisk together the milk, sour cream, and cheese. Add the tamari and pepper.

Add the onions and bring to a boil. Add the tarragon and simmer on low for 10 minutes.

Brown Rice

Serves 6

3 cups	water
¼ cup	chopped yellow onion
1 tablespoon	tamari
½ teaspoon	celery seed
	dash of sea salt
1½ cups	brown rice, washed

Bring water, onion, tamari, celery seed, and salt to a boil in a stainless steel pot.

Add the brown rice. Cover the pot and again bring to a boil. Reduce heat to medium and cook 30 minutes, then remove from the heat and allow to steam an additional 10 minutes. Do not lift the lid.

Crunchy Cornbread

Serves 8

1½ cups	cornmeal
½ cup	whole-wheat flour
1	yellow onion, chopped
1 ear	of corn, cut off cob
1 teaspoon	sea salt
1 tablespoon	lemon juice
¾ cup	oat milk
¼ cup	corn syrup
½ teaspoon	baking soda
¼ cup	corn oil

Preheat the oven to 400°F.

Mix all the ingredients in a large bowl. Grease an 8-inch-square pan. Spread the batter evenly in the pan. Bake for 40 minutes, or until toothpick comes out clean.

Curried Basmati Rice

Serves 8

2 cups	basmati rice
4 cups	water
2 tablespoons	green cardamom seeds
3 teaspoons	vegetable margarine
½ cup	finely chopped yellow onion
2	garlic cloves, minced
½ teaspoon	grated ginger root
2	bay leaves
½ teaspoon	each cumin, turmeric, cinnamon, cayenne pepper, and coriander
½ cup	cooked chickpeas
4 tablespoons	chopped fresh mint
¼ cup	slivered almonds

Soak the rice in water for one hour then rinse. Cover with 4 cups of water and bring to a boil. Reduce the heat, add the cardamom seeds and simmer 20 minutes. (Alternatively, use a rice cooker.)

Melt the margarine in a saucepan and sauté the onion in it. Add the garlic, ginger, bay leaves, and spices. Add the mixture to the cooked rice, mixing well.

Fold in the chickpeas, mint, and almonds.

Curried Coconut Rice

Serves 8

2 cups	basmati rice
2 cups	water
2 cups	coconut milk
3 tablespoons	vegetable margarine
½ teaspoon	each cumin, turmeric, cinnamon, cayenne pepper, and coriander
½	leek, thinly sliced
2	garlic cloves, minced
4 teaspoons	fresh mint
4 teaspoons	grated coconut

Cover the rice with water; soak for 1 hour then rinse. Place the rice in a pan with the 2 cups of water and the coconut milk; bring to a boil. Reduce heat and simmer 20 minutes. Melt the margarine in a skillet and add the spices, leek, and garlic; sauté. Add the leek mixture to the cooked rice, mixing well. Fold in the mint and coconut.

Dinner Popovers

Serves 8

2 cups	flour
	egg replacer for 4 eggs
1 cup	oat milk
1 teaspoon	salt
6 tablespoons	safflower oil

Whisk all the ingredients together. Ladle into oiled popover pan and bake at 250° F for 35 minutes.

Pilaf au Naturel

Serves 6 plus

2 teaspoons	olive oil
½ cup	chopped yellow onion
½ cup	shredded carrots
½ cup	minced red bell pepper
2	garlic cloves, minced
2 teaspoons	curry powder
1 teaspoon	red-pepper flakes
½ teaspoon	grated ginger root
6 cups	kale, chopped
2 cups	brown rice, cooked
1 cup	quinoa, cooked
2 tablespoons	tamari
1 cup	chickpeas, cooked

Heat the oil in a skillet, add the next 8 ingredients, and sauté until the onion has softened. Add the remaining ingredients and heat thoroughly before serving.

shrimp Fried Rice

Serves 6-8

½ cup	safflower oil
1	shallot, chopped
1 slice	ginger root
¼ pound	veggie shrimp
2	scallions, sliced
¼ pound	firm tofu, diced
12	shiitake mushrooms, sliced
2 cups	cooked rice
2 teaspoons	tamari
½ teaspoon	pepper

Place ¼ cup of the oil in a skillet and add the shallot, ginger root, and veggie shrimp; fry 3 minutes. Reserve, keeping warm. In the same skillet, place the remaining oil, the scallions, tofu, and mushrooms. Fry for 4 minutes. Put aside in another bowl, and keep warm.

Place the rice in the skillet and add the tamari and pepper. Introduce the tofu mixture, then the shrimp mixture, and fry for about 4 minutes. Serve immediately.

Squash Me Risotto!

Serves 6

3 tablespoons	vegetable margarine
1	large white onion, chopped
1½ cups	arborio rice
2 tablespoons	olive oil
5 cups	vegetable broth, heated
2 cups	squash such as pumpkin, acorn or butternut, diced and cooked
½ bunch	kale, steamed and shredded
½ cup	flat-leaf parsley, minced
½ cup	shredded veggie Swiss cheese
	black pepper
	fresh parsley to garnish

Heat 2 tablespoons of the margarine in a Dutch oven. Stir in the onion and sauté 8 minutes. Add the rice and oil, stirring to coat each rice grain completely. Add ½ cup broth—the mixture will sizzle. Once it has stopped sizzling, add the squash and 1 cup of broth. Stir continuously over a medium heat and as the rice absorbs the liquid, continue to add more broth, never allowing the mixture to dry out. Do this for 20 minutes.

Stir in the kale and add more broth; cook an additional 15 minutes. Add the parsley, shredded veggie cheese, and pepper. Add the remaining tablespoon of margarine and whisk the rice well. Garnish with parsley and serve immediately.

Sticky Rice

Serves 4

2 cups	water
1½ cups	long grain white rice
1 teaspoon	sea salt
4 tablespoons	finely chopped fresh parsley

Bring the water to a boil then add the rice, salt, and parsley. Cook for 20 minutes on low heat until the water is absorbed (or use one of those inexpensive rice cookers). Mound into a bowl.

Stuffing for Tofu Turkey

Serves 8

2 teaspoons	olive oil
1	small white onion, chopped
¼ cup	diced celery
2 cups	cornbread crumbs (see Cornbread recipe page 220)
1 cup	cooked wild rice
¼ cup	walnuts
1 cup	orange juice
2 cups	vegetable broth
¼ cup	diced apple
2 tablespoons	grated lemon peel
¼ cup	diced water chestnuts
½ cup	sherry
3 tablespoons	fresh sage
1 tablespoon	fresh tarragon
2 teaspoons	sea salt
1 teaspoon	black pepper

Preheat the oven to 425° F. In a saucepan place the oil, onion, and celery; sauté.

Add the remaining ingredients and combine well. Cook in the oven for 30 minutes, or until browned.

Good served as a side with Tofu Turkey (page 133).

TJ's Greens and Beans

Serves 8

2 cups	black beans
6 cups	water
1 tablespoon	red pepper
	sea salt
1	white onion, chopped
3 tablespoons	tamari
6 cups	mustard, turnip and collard greens

Soak the beans overnight; rinse well. Bring the water to a boil, add the beans and red pepper and simmer until the beans are tender, 1–2 hours. Season halfway through cooking and then again when done, according to taste.

Bring another pan of water to a boil. Add the onion and tamari, then the greens. Cook for 30 minutes or until tender.

Serve the beans and greens with brown rice, cornbread and salsa.

Wild Rice Pilaf

Serves 8

1½ cups	basmati rice
2 teaspoons	salt
6 tablespoons	olive oil
3½ cups	vegetable broth
1	yellow onion, chopped
3 teaspoons	pine nuts
½ cup	wild rice
½ cup	vermicelli, broken into pieces
½ teaspoon	allspice
	black pepper
3 tablespoons	fresh Italian parsley

Place the basmati rice in a stockpot and cover with hot water. Add salt and allow to sit until the water cools; drain.

Heat the oil in a skillet, add the onions and sauté 3 minutes. Add the pine nuts, wild rice, and vermicelli. Allow the mixture to brown then set aside.

Pour the vegetable broth over the basmati rice and add the onions, wild rice, vermicelli, and pine nuts. Add the allspice and pepper to taste. Bring to a boil, reduce the heat to a simmer and cook for about 15 minutes until broth is absorbed. Mix in the parsley. Cover and allow to set for 15 minutes before serving.

Desserts:

SWEET BAKED GOODS, FRUITS ...

LIGHT & LUSCIOUS OR RICH AND

SINFULLY DELICIOUS!

The happy end to the meal ... divine!

14-Karat Cake
(Take Two: Carrot Cake)

Serves 8–10

Cake:

1 cup	white flour
1½ cups	whole-wheat flour
2 teaspoons	baking soda
2 teaspoons	cinnamon
¾ cup	chopped macadamia nuts
¼ cup	corn oil
1 cup	maple syrup
	egg replacer for 3 eggs
2 cups	grated carrots
Juice of 1	orange
2 teaspoons	orange zest
½ cup	crushed pineapple
2 teaspoons	vanilla extract

Frosting:

6 ounces	soy cream cheese
6 tablespoons	vegetable margarine
2⅓ cups	powdered sugar
1 teaspoon	vanilla extract
2 teaspoons	orange zest
⅓ cup	flaked coconut
⅓ cup	chopped macadamia nuts

Preheat the oven to 350°F. First prepare the cake. Combine the dry ingredients and mix in the nuts. Combine the remaining ingredients in a separate bowl. Blend the dry ingredients into the wet ingredients and pour the batter into a nonstick or greased 8-inch pan. Bake for 45–60 minutes. Cool. While the cake is cooling, combine all the frosting ingredients and beat until smooth. Ice the cake when cool.

50s Refrigerator Cheesecake Revisited

Serves 8 plus

Crust:

2 cups	graham cracker crumbs (reserve ½ cup)
½ cup	cane sugar
½ cup	vegetable margarine, melted

Topping:

½ cup	vegan gelatin or ¼ cup agar agar flakes
½ or ¼ cup	cold water (½ for the vegan gelatin, ¼ for the agar)
8 ounces	soy cream cheese
1 cup	cane sugar
¼ cup	lemon juice
½ cup	crushed pineapple
1 teaspoon	vanilla extract
¾ cup	almond milk
1 cup	non-dairy whipped topping

Mix all the crust ingredients together and press into a 9-inch spring-form pie pan or a 9- x 13-inch rectangular cake pan. Refrigerate while you prepare the topping.

Mix the gelatin or agar agar with the water and heat to dissolve. Cool. Beat the soy cheese and cane sugar, gradually adding gelatin or agar agar, lemon juice, pineapple, and vanilla. Beat the milk a little then add the cheese mixture and gelatin. Place in the refrigerator for 20 minutes to thicken.

Fold in the whipped topping. Pour over the crust and refrigerate overnight. Garnish with the reserved graham cracker crumbs mixture and lemon zest or your favorite fruit topping.

Apple Sauce Kuchen

Serves 12 plus

1¼ cups	applesauce
1 cup	raw sugar
¼ cup	safflower oil
¼ cup	veggie sour cream
1 cup	hazelnut milk
2 cups	whole-wheat flour
3 tablespoons	baking soda
2 teaspoons	cinnamon
½ teaspoon	nutmeg
¼ cup	chopped hazelnuts
½ cup	golden raisins

Preheat the oven to 350°F. Oil a 9- x 13-inch pan or a Bundt cake pan (you can use individual ones for tea time).

Combine the applesauce, sugar, oil, sour cream, and milk. Next combine the flour, soda, and spices. Add the flour mixture to the applesauce mixture and combine well. Stir in the nuts and raisins.

Pour into the baking pan and bake 40 minutes, or until toothpick comes out clean. Cool.

Serve as is or with Soy Cream Cheese Frosting (page 346) and garnish with apple slices and veggie cheddar cheese shreds. And how about serving on an apple sauce "splash"...

Carob Beetroot Cake

Serves 12

4 ounces	carob or cocoa powder
1 cup	vegetable oil
2½ cups	raw sugar
2 cups	shredded beets
2 tablespoons	vanilla extract
2 cups	whole-wheat or all-purpose flour
	egg replacer for 3 eggs
4 teaspoons	baking powder
1 teaspoon	baking soda
¼ teaspoon	sea salt

Preheat the oven to 350°F.

Place the carob and oil in a double boiler and heat until melted. Mix together the dry ingredients. Now combine all the ingredients, folding in the beets.

Place the batter in an oiled Bundt (tube) pan. Bake for 1 hour. Cool then dust with powdered sugar or drizzle with a vegan glaze.

German Chocolate Cake

Serves 12

Cake:
6 ounces	dried fruit (apple, apricot and date is good)
¾ cup	purified water
	egg replacer for 3 eggs
3 cups	raw sugar
1¼ cups	carob or cocoa powder
3 cups	white flour
3 teaspoons	baking soda
2 teaspoons	baking powder
2 cups	oat or almond milk
3 teaspoons	white vinegar
2 teaspoons	vanilla extract

Icing:
2 cups	oat milk
2 teaspoons	vanilla extract
2 cups	raw sugar
5 tablespoons	arrowroot
¾ cup	water
2 cups	flaked coconut
2 cups	chopped walnuts

Soak the dried fruit in the water until softened then puree it. Mix the puree with the egg replacer and sugar. Mix together the dry ingredients and add to the fruit puree.

Combine the milk, vinegar, and vanilla. Add this to the fruit puree. Allow it to rest for 15 minutes.

Preheat oven to 350°F. Oil and flour 3 x 8-inch cake pans. Divide the batter evenly between them. Bake for 30 minutes, or until toothpick comes out clean.

Cool, and remove the cakes from the pans.

While the cake is cooling, make the icing. Combine the milk, vanilla, and sugar in a saucepan and bring to a boil. Mix the arrowroot and water. Stir this into the milk mixture and allow it to thicken. Add the coconut and nuts. Allow the icing to cool before decorating the cake.

Pineapple Right-Side-Up Cake

Serves 8

½ cup	whole blanched almonds
4 tablespoons	vegetable margarine, melted
½ cup	maple syrup
½	fresh pineapple, trimmed and sliced into rings
3	ripe plums, halved and quartered
1½ cups	whole-wheat pastry flour
½ cup	raw sugar
¾ teaspoon	baking powder
¼ teaspoon	baking soda
½ teaspoon	sea salt
9 tablespoons	vegetable margarine, softened
½ cup	veggie sour cream
1 teaspoon	vanilla extract

Preheat the oven to 350°F. Toast the almonds on a cookie sheet for 15 minutes. Set aside. Turn the oven down to 325°F.

Combine the melted margarine and maple syrup use to coat bottom and sides of a 10-inch ovenproof glass dish. Arrange the pineapple slices on the bottom of the dish and place a quartered plum in each pineapple slice, cut side up. Place the almonds on top.

Mix the dry ingredients. Using a mixer, combine the softened margarine, sour cream, and vanilla in a large bowl. Add the dry ingredients and beat for about 2 minutes on medium speed until smooth. Spread the mixture evenly over the pineapple. Bake for 40–50 minutes, or until brown and a toothpick comes out clean. Allow it to cool for 5 minutes then transfer to a cake plate.

Polenta Pound Cake

Serves 8 plus

1½ cups	all-purpose flour
1 cup	cornmeal
1½ teaspoons	baking powder
¼ cup	vegetable margarine
¾ cup	brown sugar
¾ cup	raw sugar
¾ cup	tofu
1 teaspoon	vanilla extract
Dash of	almond extract
Dash of	sea salt
	egg replacer for 5 eggs
	powdered sugar

Preheat the oven to 350°F. Grease a 9 x 5 inch baking dish or loaf pan and dust with flour.

Mix the flour, cornmeal, and baking powder. Set aside.

In a large bowl, beat the margarine and sugars until combined. Add the tofu, salt, and extracts. Add the egg replacer and mix well. Now add the dry ingredients and stir until just combined. Bake for 60–70 minutes, or until a toothpick comes out clean. Cool for 10 minutes then invert and give it a blast of powdered sugar.

Great served with Pears in Lemon Syrup (page 283).

Grand Marnier Special

Serves 8

2 cups	orange juice
1	vanilla bean
4	oranges, sliced
1 cup	Syrah wine
1 cup	soy cream cheese
1 cup	Grand Marnier liqueur
1	Polenta Pound Cake (page 239)
4 teaspoons	orange zest

Place the orange juice in a saucepan, scrape the contents of the vanilla bean into it and bring to a boil. Reduce the heat and add half the orange slices and the wine; continue to heat until the mixture thickens and is reduced by half.

Beat together the soy cream cheese and liqueur.

Cut eight slices of pound cake. Arrange remaining orange slices on the cake slices and spoon the soy cheese over the top. Repeat with the vanilla Syrah. Sprinkle the zest over the top.

Tofu Cheesecake

Serves 12 or more

1	cheesecake crust (see 50s Refrigerator Cheesecake page 233)
10-ounce package	regular tofu
3 x 8-oz packages	soy cream cheese
¼ cup	lemon juice*
2 tablespoons	vanilla extract
2 cup	maple syrup
½ cup	veggie sour cream
2 tablespoons	arrowroot

Preheat the oven to 350°F. Prepare the crust according recipe instructions. Press into an oiled spring-form pan and up sides of pan. Bake 8 minutes and cool.

Combine the remaining ingredients. Pour into the cake pan and bake for 2–3 hours, checking every 15 minutes or so, until set and lightly browned. Cool, remove from pan and chill overnight. Place your favorite fruit or topping on top: strawberries, raspberries, blueberries, cherries, mangoes, pineapple, kiwifruit, limes, oranges, melon, "cream" toppings, banana nut caramel, liqueur infusions, carob garnishes, etc.

* You can substitute your favorite "flavoring" for half of the lemon juice to create a specialty cheesecake.

Pumpkin Spice Loaf

Serves 10

2 cups	pureed pumpkin
½ cup	corn oil
¼ cup	silken tofu
1	large apple, peeled, cored, and grated
1 cup	brown sugar
2 cups	all-purpose flour
1 teaspoon	baking soda
½ teaspoon	baking powder
¼ teaspoon	salt
½ teaspoon	cinnamon
½ teaspoon	nutmeg
½ cup	golden raisins
½ cup	chopped pecans

Preheat the oven to 350° F. Grease a loaf pan.

Mix the wet ingredients together; do the same for the dry. Combine the two. Pour the mixture into the loaf pan and bake for 50–60 minutes. Cool. Serve plain or with Brandied Cream Sauce (page 345).

Zuckerman's Peach Glaze

Yields 1 cup

2	peaches, peeled and pureed
1 cup	corn syrup
½ teaspoon	limejuice
4 teaspoons	arrowroot
2 teaspoon	vegetable shortening

Place the peaches in a saucepan with the syrup; bring to a boil then reduce the heat and simmer 4 minutes. Add the limejuice and arrowroot, stirring until thickened. Remove from the heat. Add the shortening and mix well. Cool until barely warm.

Pour over chilled or frozen desserts such as sorbet, tofu cheesecake, etc. Put the glazed desserts into the freezer or refrigerator until firm. Garnish with fruit syrup and accompany with fruit slices, carob sauce ... as you wish!

Carob-and-Vanilla-Coated Pretzel Sticks

Serves 4

2 ounces	carob chips plus 1 teaspoon vegetable shortening
2 ounces	vanilla chips plus 1 teaspoon vegetable shortening
4 ounces bag	organic salted pretzel sticks

Line a cookie sheet with waxed paper. Melt the carob chips and shortening in a double boiler. Dip in pretzel sticks, coating evenly. Place on lined sheet and allow to set.

Repeat with the vanilla chips and shortening.

Great garnished with Vanilla Carob Glace (page 299).

Fantastic Fudge

Yields 2–3 dozen pieces depending upon how you cut it

6 tablespoons	vegetable margarine
3½ cups	powdered sugar
½ cup	cocoa powder
1 teaspoon	vanilla extract
¼ cup	oat milk
1 cup	chopped walnuts

Grease a 5 x 9-inch baking pan.

Place all the ingredients, except the nuts, in a double boiler, and stir until smooth. Add the nuts. Pour into the greased pan. Chill and cut. (I like to use a cookie cutter and make different shapes!)

Hazelnut Lace Cradles

Yields at least 8 cradles

2 cups	hazelnuts*
½ cup	raw sugar
2 tablespoons	all-purpose flour
¼ teaspoon	sea salt
¼ cup	vegetable margarine
2 tablespoons	almond milk

Process the hazelnuts, sugar, flour, and salt.

Melt the margarine and then add milk. Stir this into the nut mixture. Transfer the dough to a bowl and refrigerate 1 to 24 hours.

Preheat the oven to 300°F.

Line a cookie sheet with parchment and place teaspoons of the dough on it, 4 inches apart. Place another piece of parchment over the cookies and press down. Finish flattening them with a rolling pin, reducing the thickness to paper thin. Bake in the oven until golden brown, about 15 minutes.

Remove from the oven and quickly mold into desired form. Use a rolling pin for cradles or boats, a muffin tin for cups, spice jars for bowls ... Allow the cookies to cool completely then remove the mold. Fill with your favorite mousse, cheesecake, or sorbet. Garnish and serve.

*You can substitute almonds or macadamia nuts for the hazelnuts.

No-Bake Kids' Treats

Yields 4 dozen treats

2 cups	cane sugar
1 teaspoon	salt
8 tablespoons	cocoa
1 cup	carob or peanut chips
1 tablespoon	oat milk
¾ cup	vegetable margarine
3 cups	quick-cook rolled oats
1 cup	flaked coconut or favorite trail mix

Combine the sugar, salt, and cocoa in double boiler. Add the margarine and chips. Stir continuously as you bring it to a boil. Add the oats and coconut or trail mix. If the mixture is too stiff add oat milk. Drop teaspoonfuls of the mixture onto wax paper and leave to rest until set.

Nutty Cocoa Truffles

Yields about 5 dozen

10 ounces	soy cream cheese
3 cups	powdered sugar
12 ounces	carob chips, melted
2 teaspoons	vanilla extract
	ground nuts and cocoa powder

Beat the cream cheese until smooth. Blend in the powdered sugar then add the carob chips and vanilla. Refrigerate for one hour. Form into balls and roll in the nuts and cocoa. Store in the refrigerator.

Trail Mix Toffee

Yields about 24 pieces

½ cup	vegetable margarine
1 cup	raw sugar (½ brown and ½ white)
¼ cup	grated carob
1 cup	maple syrup
¼ cup	trail mix (no fruit)
¼ teaspoon	vanilla extract

Melt the margarine in a medium saucepan and add the sugar, carob, and maple syrup. Bring to a boil and boil for 15 minutes. The mixture will form hard threads in cold water when tested (280°F on a candy thermometer). Stir in the trail mix and vanilla. Pour the mixture into a greased dish and spread evenly. Mark into squares when cool and break into pieces when cold. Store in an airtight container.

Turtles Rule!

Yields 24

¼ pound	pecan halves
24	vegan caramels, unwrapped
1 cup	carob chips
1 teaspoon	vegetable shortening

Preheat the oven to 350°F. On a cookie sheet arrange 3 pecans in a "Y" shape. Place a caramel in the center of each "Y" shape. Bake until melted, 5 minutes or so. Place the carob chips and shortening in a double boiler and melt. Mix well and spread over candies. Refrigerate for 45 minutes to 1 hour.

Blondies

Yields 16 bars

2 cups	flour
2 cups	brown sugar
1 teaspoon	baking powder
1 cup	vegetable oil
1 cup	water
1 teaspoon	vanilla extract
½ cup	vegan butterscotch chips
¼ cup	chopped macadamia nuts

Preheat the oven to 350°F. Coat a 9 x 13-inch baking pan with vegetable cooking spray.

Mix the flour, sugar, and baking powder together. Stir in the oil, water, and vanilla, mixing well. Fold in the chips and nuts. Spread the batter in the pan and bake until light brown, about 30 minutes. Allow it to cool for 10 minutes before cutting into bars.

Brownies

Yields 12 plus

2 cups	flour
½ cup	cocoa
2 cups	raw sugar
1 teaspoon	baking powder
½ teaspoon	sea salt
¼ cup	chopped nuts
¼ cup	carob chips
1 cup	vegetable oil
1 teaspoon	vanilla extract
1 cup	veggie sour cream

Preheat the oven to 350°F. Spray a 9 x 13 inch baking pan with vegetable cooking spray.

Combine the dry ingredients in a large bowl. Combine the liquid ingredients. Add the liquid ingredients to the dry ingredients and combine. Spread the batter in the pan. Bake for 40 minutes, or until the edges are firm and the center is set. Allow to cool for 10 minutes before cutting.

Cranberry Oatmeal Drops

Yields about 20 cookies

1 cup	vegetable margarine
¾ cup	raw sugar
	egg replacer for one egg
1½ teaspoons	vanilla extract
½ teaspoon	salt
1 cup	wheat flour
¾ teaspoon	baking powder
1½ cups	rolled oats
¾ cup	dried cranberries
¾ cup	chopped almonds
¼ cup	almond milk

Preheat the oven to 375°F.

Mix all the ingredients together, except the milk. Once combined, add enough milk to bind the ingredients.

Form into balls, place on a greased cookie sheet, and flatten each ball a little using a fork. Bake for 12 minutes.

Double Peanut Oat Drops

Yields about 4 dozen

1 cup	vegetable margarine
1 cup	brown sugar
½ cup	raw sugar
	egg replacer for 2 eggs
1 teaspoon	vanilla extract
1 teaspoon	cinnamon
½ teaspoon	sea salt
½ teaspoon	baking soda
½ teaspoon	baking powder
1½ cups	all-purpose flour
2 cups	oatmeal
½ cup	peanut butter chips
1 cup	chopped peanuts

Preheat oven to 350°F.

Cream the margarine and sugars together in a large bowl. Add the egg replacer and vanilla. Mix the remaining ingredients together, except the chips and nuts then add to the sugar mixture. Mix in the chips and nuts last.

Drop by tablespoon onto a greased cookie sheet and bake for about 12 minutes.

Grand Munchies

Yields 24 cookies

3 cups	whole-wheat flour
½ cup	oatmeal
3 tablespoons	baking powder
1 tablespoon	baking soda
½ teaspoon	sea salt
¾ cup	maple syrup
¾ cup	apple juice
½ cup	sunflower oil
2 teaspoons	vanilla extract
¼ cup	carob chips
¼ cup	dried fruit, diced
¼ cup	pecans or macadamia nuts, chopped

Preheat the oven to 425°F.

Combine the wheat flour, oatmeal, baking powder, soda, and salt in a large bowl; mix well. Add the syrup, apple juice, oil, and vanilla; mix well. Combine the chips, fruit, and nuts; add to the flour mixture. You should now have a coarse and doughy mixture.

Brush a cookie sheet with 2 tablespoons sunflower oil.

Flour your hands and form the dough into golf-ball-size balls and place on cookie sheet.

Bake 8 minutes.

Luscious Lemon Bars

Yields 24 bars

Crust:

1 cup	crispy rice cereal, crushed
½ cup	vegetable margarine
¼ cup	powdered sugar

Filling:

	egg replacer for 2 eggs
2 tablespoons	lemon juice
1 cup	cane sugar
½ teaspoon	baking powder
2½ tablespoons	flour

Topping:

¾ cup	powdered sugar
½ teaspoon	vanilla extract
1 tablespoon	vegetable margarine
½ tablespoon	rice milk
½ teaspoon	lemon zest

Preheat the oven to 350°F.

Grease an 8-inch-square x 2-inch-deep pan.

Mix the crust ingredients together and press into the pan. Combine the filling ingredients and pour over the crust. Bake for 20 minutes.

Mix the topping ingredients together, spread over the warm bars, and sprinkle with zest. Cut and serve.

Not Your Ordinary
Rice Krisp Squares

Yields 24 bars

12 ounces	carob chips
6 ounces	vegan butterscotch chips
½ cup	vegetable margarine
1 cup	peanut butter
3 cups	rice krisp cereal
2 cups	vegan marshmallows
½ cup	chopped cashews

Melt the carob and butterscotch chips, margarine, and peanut butter in a double boiler. Add the rice cereal, marshmallows, and cashews. Stir to combine and press the mixture into a greased 9 x 13 inch pan. Set aside to cool and cut when cool.

Pineapple Banana Biscotti

Yields 24 cookies

2	ripe bananas, mashed
½ cup	crushed pineapple
½ cup	almond milk
2 cups	flour (your choice)
1 teaspoon	baking soda
¼ cup	raw sugar
1 teaspoon	cinnamon
¼ cup	vegetable margarine, melted
2 tablespoons	egg replacer
	powdered sugar

Preheat the oven to 350°F. Line a cookie sheet with aluminum foil or oil the sheet.

Mix all ingredients together to form a sticky dough*. Pour out onto a lightly floured work surface and roll the dough into a ball, adding flour as necessary to prevent it sticking to the surface. Place the dough on the cookie sheet, forming it into a large loaf. Flatten the top and bake 30 minutes.

Remove from the oven and cut the loaf, crosswise, into ¾-inch-thick slices. Place the slices back on the cookie sheet upright to resemble a loaf and return to the oven. Bake an additional 15 minutes. Sprinkle with powdered sugar. Serve with tea or coffee.

* For variety add ¼ cup chopped nuts, dried cherries, or vanilla chips.

Tell-My-Fortune Cookies

Yields 12 cookies

	egg replacer for 1 egg
⅓ cup	cane sugar
2 tablespoons	safflower oil
2 tablespoons	water
¼ cup	cornstarch
3 drops	almond extract
12	fortunes

Preheat the oven to 350°F. Beat the "egg" then add the sugar and beat until the mixture is very thick. Fold in the oil. In a medium bowl, mix the water with the cornstarch. Now add the "egg" batter, a little at a time, until it is completely incorporated. Add the extract.

Drop the batter, a tablespoon at a time, onto a cookie sheet and bake until the edges are light brown, about 4 minutes. Lift one cookie at a time and flip over. Lay the "fortune" in the center and fold the cookie in half over it. Fold the cookie in half again to form a fortune cookie shape. Place in a muffin tray or bowl so that it holds its shape while cooling. Repeat with the remaining batter.

Vegan Drop Cookies

Yields 12 cookies

1 cup	vegan mayonnaise dressing
¾ cup	raw sugar
¼ cup	maple syrup
1 teaspoon	vanilla extract
1 teaspoon	baking soda
2 cups	all purpose flour
½ teaspoon	sea salt
	extra raw sugar for coating

Combine all the ingredients in a bowl. Turn out onto a work surface, break into 12 pieces and roll into balls. Roll in the raw sugar. Place on a lightly oiled cookie sheet and press flat with a spoon. If you wish, add a roasted nutmeat of your choice, or lightly brush with more maple syrup. Bake at 350°F for 12 minutes.

Winter Pecan Logs

Yields 2 dozen

½ cup	vegetable margarine, softened
4 ounces	soy cream cheese
1 teaspoon	vanilla extract
1¾ cups	all-purpose flour
1 tablespoon	raw sugar
Dash of	salt
1 cup	chopped pecans
	cocoa powder or powdered sugar

Preheat oven to 375°F.

Cream the vegetable margarine and soy cream cheese. Beat in the vanilla.

Mix the flour, sugar, and salt in a large bowl. Add the cheese mixture and fold in the pecans. Turn out of the bowl onto a work surface and shape into small logs. Place on an oiled cookie sheet and bake 12 minutes. Roll in the cocoa powder or powdered sugar.

Amaretto Silk Pie

Serves 8

Crust:

¼ cup	cane sugar
¼ cup	ground almonds
½ cup	graham cracker crumbs
¼ teaspoon	sea salt
Juice of ½	lemon
1 tablespoon	cinnamon
½ cup	vegetable margarine, melted

Filling:

1 pound	tofu
¾ cup	powdered sugar
¾ cup	safflower oil
¾ teaspoon	tamari
6 tablespoons	vanilla extract
2 shots	organic amaretto liqueur

Topping:

2 cups	non-dairy whipped topping
	slivered almonds

First make the crust. Mix the sugar, almonds, graham cracker crumbs, and salt in a bowl. Add the lemon juice, cinnamon, and margarine. Combine and press into a 9-inch pie pan, taking the crust up the sides. Bake at 350°F for 15 minutes. Cool.

To make the filling, simply blend all the filling ingredients in a food processor until smooth. Pour into crust. Refrigerate for 3 hours or overnight. Top with non-dairy whipped topping (flavored with ½ shot of Amaretto) and garnish with the almonds.

For an alternative, spoon the filling into glasses, alternating with layers of non-diary whipped topping, and top with almonds.

Apple Pie

Serves 8–10

1 cup	maple syrup
¼ cup	vegetable margarine, melted
3 teaspoons	cinnamon
6	medium granny smith apples, sliced
6	medium macintosh apples, sliced
2 teaspoons	allspice
2 teaspoons	nutmeg
½ teaspoon	cloves
Juice of 1	lemon
3 tablespoons	whole-wheat flour
2	Gourmet Whole-Wheat Pie Crusts, unbaked (page 266)

Preheat the oven to 350°F.

Mix 1 teaspoon of syrup, 1 teaspoon of vegetable margarine, and ½ teaspoon cinnamon; set aside.

Combine the apples, spices, margarine, syrup, and lemon juice. Add the flour. Arrange the mixture in the bottom of a piecrust. Place the second crust over the apples and crimp the edges. Brush the top of the piecrust with the reserved spice-and-syrup mixture. Bake until bubbly and the crust is browned, 50–55 minutes.

Serve warm. It's great with veggie cheddar cheese slices.

Carob Mocha Silk Pie

Serves 8

Crust:

¼ cup	raw sugar
¼ cup	ground hazelnuts
½ cup	graham cracker crumbs
¼ teaspoon	sea salt
Juice of ½	lemon
1 tablespoon	instant coffee
4 tablespoons	vegetable margarine, melted

Filling:

1 pound	tofu
¾ cup	powdered sugar
¾ cup	safflower oil
¾ teaspoon	tamari
1 tablespoon	vanilla extract
6 tablespoons	carob powder
1 shot	Kahlúa liqueur

Topping:

2 cups	non-dairy whipped topping
	chopped hazelnuts and carob chips

First make the crust. Mix the sugar, hazelnuts, graham cracker crumbs, and salt in a bowl. Add the lemon juice, coffee, and margarine. Combine and press into a 9-inch pie pan, taking the crust up the sides. Bake at 350°F for 15 minutes. Cool.

To make the filling, simply blend all the filling ingredients in a food processor until smooth. Pour into the crust. Refrigerate 3 hours or overnight. Top with the whipped topping (flavored with ½ shot of Kahlua) and garnish with the hazelnuts and carob chips.

Cherry Chiffon Pie

Serves 8 plus

2 cups	bing cherries, pitted
½ cup	cane sugar
½ cup	water
4 tablespoons	cornstarch
¼ cup	cherry liqueur
3 cups	whipped non-dairy topping
1	pie crust (see 50s Refrigerator Cheesecake recipe page 233)
½ cup	white carob shavings

Place the cherries, sugar, and water in a saucepan. Stir over medium to high heat until boiling and the sugar is dissolved. Add the cornstarch and allow the mixture to thicken.

Remove from the heat and mix in the liqueur. Cool.

Fold in the whipped topping and mound into the piecrust. Garnish with carob shavings. Refrigerate for 4 hours before serving.

Crumb Pie Shell

Yields 1 piecrust

1 cup	vegetable margarine, melted
½ cup	raw sugar
¼ cup	graham cracker crumbs
¼ teaspoon	sea salt
3 tablespoons	wheat flour
2 tablespoons	cinnamon

Combine all the ingredients in a bowl. Turn the moist mixture into a pie dish and, using the back of a spoon, press it into the dish, spreading evenly to cover the base and sides to about a ¼-inch thickness. Bake at 325° F for 8 minutes.

Four Seasons Fruit Tart

Serves 8

Pastry:

2 cups	whole-wheat or all-purpose flour
½ cup	vegetable oil
Pinch of	salt
½	cold water

Fruit Filling:

5	bartlett pears, peeled and sliced
3 tablespoons	corn oil
1	vanilla bean
1 cup	karo syrup
3 tablespoons	cinnamon
2 tablespoons	flour
1 cup	blueberries

First make the pastry case. Combine the flour, oil, and salt in a large bowl. Slowly add the cold water, working the mixture to a dough. Refrigerate 10 minutes. Roll out on a floured surface until large enough to fit a standard tart pan. Transfer to a tart pan and line the shell with parchment. Fill the tart with dried beans. Bake at 350°F for 10–12 minutes. Remove from the oven, empty the tart and trim the edges. Wait 5 minutes then remove the shell from the pan.

While the pastry is cooking, place pears, oil, and vanilla bean in a saucepan and cook over medium heat for about 4 minutes, until pears are tender. Remove the vanilla bean and add the karo and cinnamon. Lower the heat and cook until caramelized, about 6 minutes longer. Add the flour and allow the mixture to thicken. Fold in the blueberries, stir for 1 minute then remove from heat. Fill the tart with the fruit mixture ... and voilà!

Great served with Vanilla Carob Glace (page 299).

Gourmet Whole-Wheat Piecrust

Makes 1 double 10-inch crust or 2 single crusts

2 cups	whole-wheat pastry flour
¼ cup	white cornmeal
¼ cup	chopped hazelnuts
1 teaspoon	sea salt
½ cup	vegetable margarine, melted
½ cup	ice water

Combine the dry ingredients in a bowl. Add the margarine and mix in well. Add the water and mix to a dough. Divide in half and form into two balls using your hands.

Roll out on wax paper and transfer to an oiled pie pan/s.

Crimp the edges and, if you are placing one of the shells over a filling, aerate the top of shell 2–3 times with fork. Bake the piecrusts at 350°F until browned, about 10 minutes.

Hot Cherry Pies

12 mini pies

2 pounds	bing cherries, pitted
2 cups	cane sugar
1 cup	water
1 cup	organic marsala
2 tablespoons	flour mixed with enough water to form paste
12	large spring roll wrappers
	safflower oil

In a saucepan, combine the cherries with the sugar and water. Bring to a boil, stirring to dissolve the sugar. Add the wine and allow to thicken. Remove from heat and leave to cool completely.

Lay out the wrappers and divide the cherry filling between them. Fold each wrapper over its filling and use the flour and water paste to seal. Fry in oil for 3 minutes or until golden. Drain on a rack and serve warm.

McD's ... take a back seat!

Peach Blueberry Cobbler

Serves 8

4 cups	peaches, pitted, peeled, and cut into ½-inch slices
1 cup	blueberries
⅔ cup	raw sugar
2 tablespoons	wheat flour
3 teaspoons	grated lemon peel

Topping:

1½ cups	wheat flour
¼ teaspoon	sea salt
1 tablespoon	baking powder
2 tablespoons	raw sugar
4 tablespoons	vegetable margarine
1 cup	almond milk

Preheat the oven to 375° F. Mix the peaches and blueberries with the sugar, flour, and lemon peel. Place the mixture in a greased, square baking dish.

Mix the topping ingredients together and pour over the fruit. Bake for 35– 40 minutes until the fruit is bubbly and topping is browned.

Serve plain or topped with Vanilla Carob Glace (page 299).

Peanut Butter Chiffon Pie

Serves 8

1	**Crumb Pie Shell (page 264)**
1½ cups	**crunchy peanut butter**
¼ cup	**hickory syrup**
3 cups	**non-dairy whipped topping**

Preheat the oven to 325°F. Bake the pie shell for 8 minutes then allow to cool.

Combine the peanut butter and syrup then fold in the whipped topping. Spoon the mixture into the pie shell. Refrigerate for 1 hour.

Garnish with 3 tablespoons of chopped peanuts if desired.

Simple Pumpkin Pie

Serves 8

Filling:

2½ cups	pumpkin
1 teaspoon	nutmeg
2 tablespoons	cinnamon
1 teaspoon	allspice
¾ cup	oat milk
¼ cup	orange juice
1 teaspoon	grated orange peel
½ cup	karo syrup
1	unbaked Whole-Wheat Pie Crust (page 266)

Preheat the oven to 350°F.

Blend all the filling ingredients together until smooth. Place in the pie shell and bake 1–1½ hours, checking every 10 minutes, until set and a toothpick comes out clean. Cool and serve with a dollop of non-dairy whipped topping.

Strawberry Dream Pie

Serves 8

1	unbaked Gourmet Whole-Wheat Pie Crust (page 266)
3 pints	fresh strawberries, washed and stems removed
8 ounces	non-dairy whipped topping
½ cup	karo syrup
1 teaspoon	vanilla extract

Preheat oven to 375°F. Bake piecrust 10 minutes then cool.

Cut half the strawberries into slices and leave the other half whole. Reserve 4 tablespoons of the topping and combine the remainder with the sliced berries. Spread on the bottom of the cooled shell. Mix the whole berries, syrup, and vanilla. Pile into the pie shell on top of the sliced berries and topping mixture. Garnish the top with remaining topping. Refrigerate 1 hour.

Sweet Potato Pecan Pie

Serves 8

1	Whole-Wheat Pie Crust (page 266)
3 cups	sweet potatoes, skins removed, cooked and mashed
½ cup	almond milk
¾ cup	maple syrup
1 teaspoon	cinnamon
½ teaspoon	ground cloves
½ teaspoon	salt
¼ teaspoon	ginger
½ cup	chopped pecans
	non-dairy whipped topping

Preheat the oven to 350°F. Pre-bake the pie shell 10 minutes.

Mix the sweet potatoes with the milk and syrup. Combine the cinnamon, cloves, ginger, and salt; stir together and then continue blending with mixer until smooth. Cut in the pecans. Place the mixture in the pie shell. Bake for 1 hour.

Cool and garnish with the non-dairy topping.

Tanta Emma's Blueberries and Cream Tart

Serves 8

1 cup	whole-wheat or all-purpose flour
½ teaspoon	sea salt
¼ cup	vegetable margarine, chilled and cut into pieces
3 tablespoons	cold water
1½ cups	firm tofu, drained well
½ cup	cane sugar
1 teaspoon	vanilla extract
2 cups	blueberries
½ cup	blueberry preserves

Preheat the oven to 375° F.

Mix the flour and salt and process with the margarine until crumbly. Add the water, a little at a time, and process until the mixture forms a ball of dough. Turn out onto a floured surface and roll out into a 10-inch circle. Place in a 9-inch tart pan and bake until browned, about 10 minutes.

Reduce oven temperature to 350° F.

Process the tofu, sugar, and vanilla. Pour into tart and bake for 30 minutes until set. Arrange the fruit on top of the tart. Puree the preserves and pour over the berries. Refrigerate 1 hour.

For added fun, try peaches, strawberries, kiwifruit, cherries, or a combination of fruits, and add 1 tablespoon berry liqueur to the preserves.

Tropical Tartlet with Banana Cream

Serves 8

10	large apricots, peeled and sliced
4	mangoes, peeled and pureed
½ cup	karo syrup
1 teaspoon	allspice
2 teaspoons	rum
1 teaspoon	vanilla extract
1	Gourmet Whole-Wheat Pie Crust (page 266)
8 teaspoons	vegetable margarine

Banana Cream:

2	ripe bananas, mashed
½ teaspoon	lemon juice
2 cups	non-dairy whipped topping

Preheat the oven to 375° F.

Mix the apricots, mangoes, syrup, allspice, rum, and vanilla. Roll out the pie crust and cut into 8 wedges. Baste with 4 teaspoons of margarine. Place the fruit filling in the centers of the wedges and roll up, crimping the pastry edges to seal. Place on a cookie sheet oiled with the remaining margarine. Bake for 30 minutes, or until browned and bubbly. Cool.

Fold together the bananas, lemon juice, and whipped topping. Refrigerate. Serve the warm tartlets with the banana cream on the side.

You could also make one large tart, mound the "cream" on top and garnish with dried apricots...

Banana Bake

Serves 4

4 tablespoons	lemon juice
4 tablespoons	maple syrup
4	bananas, peeled and sliced
4 tablespoons	whipped non-dairy topping
½ teaspoon	vanilla extract
4	Veganaise cookies

Preheat the oven to 400°F.

Mix the lemon juice and syrup; pour over the bananas. Place in a greased ovenproof dish and bake for 10 minutes. Fold the whipped topping and vanilla together. Top the bananas with the mixture and serve with a Veganaise cookie. Drizzle with more syrup if desired.

Banana Flambé

Serves 2

2 tablespoons	vegetable margarine
2	bananas, cut lengthwise in half
Dash of	cinnamon
Dash of	nutmeg
2 tablespoons	golden raisins
1 cup	cognac
2 teaspoons	minced hazelnuts
1 tablespoon	shredded coconut

Melt the vegetable margarine in a skillet, add the bananas, and brown. Sprinkle with spices and add raisins. Reduce heat and add cognac; set alight. Once the alcohol burns off remove from the heat.

Garnish with the coconut and hazelnuts.

Great served with Vanilla Carob Glace (page 299).

Celestial Fresh Fruit Fondue

Serves 8 or more

12	each fresh strawberries, pineapple chunks, banana slices, and cherries
48	toothpicks
½ cup	finely chopped nuts or flaked coconut or a mixture of the two
8 ounces	carob chips
½ cup	soy milk
4 tablespoons	port
4 tablespoons	vegetable shortening
2 tablespoons	corn syrup

Wash the fruit and skewer onto toothpicks. Place the nuts in shallow dish.

Combine the carob chips and milk; melt. Add the port, shortening, and corn syrup. Mix until smooth.

Dip the fruit into the fondue and sprinkle with nuts. Do you hear the choir? Yum-yum!

Chai-Poached Asian Pears in Amaretto Syrup

Serves 4

4	asian pears, cored and peeled
4	cinnamon sticks
2 cups	chai green tea
1 cup	amaretto
1 cup	raw sugar
2 teaspoons	arrowroot
½ cup	slivered almonds

Set the pears upright in a small saucepan, with the cinnamon stick in the center. Pour the tea over the pears and place the pot on a medium heat. Allow it to come to a boil then reduce the heat and cover. Cook until the pears are soft, 15 minutes or so.

In small saucepan, bring the amaretto and sugar to a boil. Mix the arrowroot with 2 teaspoons of water, add to the pan, and stir to thicken.

Remove the pears from the pan, set on plates, pour some sauce over each and garnish with almonds.

Gertie's Apple Crisp

Serves 8

6	medium golden delicious apples
6	large granny smith apples
1½ teaspoons	allspice
4 teaspoons	cinnamon
2 teaspoons	nutmeg
3 tablespoons	wheat flour
1 cup	oatmeal
½ cup	maple syrup
¼ cup	raw cane sugar
½ cup	vegetable margarine, melted

Preheat the oven to 375°F.

Core the apples and slice them, leaving the skins on.

Mix the syrup, 1 teaspoon of the allspice, 3 teaspoons of the cinnamon, the nutmeg and wheat flour; combine with the apples. Brush the sides and bottom of a rectangular baking dish with 2 tablespoons vegetable margarine. Place the apples in the dish, layer by layer until finished.

Combine the remaining ½ teaspoon allspice and 1 teaspoon cinnamon with the oatmeal, sugar, and margarine. Spoon the crumbly mixture over the apples. Bake for 50 minutes or until the apples are bubbly and the topping has browned.

Gingered Plantains

Serves 4

1 cup	water
1 cup	raw sugar
2 tablespoons	grated ginger root
2 teaspoons	vegetable margarine, melted
1 cup	white wine
4	plantains
2 tablespoons	five-spice powder
½ cup	rum
4 tablespoons	fresh grated coconut

Heat the water, sugar, and ginger in a saucepan. Bring to a boil and then reduce the heat. Add the wine and continue to heat until the sauce is reduced by half.

Place the melted margarine, bananas, and five-spice in a skillet; brown 3 minutes then add the rum. Set it alight and allow the alcohol to burn off. Add the ginger sauce and heat an additional 1 minute.

Serve over plain cake and sprinkle with the coconut.

Palos Verdes Pears

Serves 4

2 ounces	**soy cream cheese**
12	**pitted bing cherries, cut in half**
4	**small ripe pears, cut in half, peeled, and cored**
2 tablespoons	**vegetable margarine, melted**
1 tablespoon	**hickory syrup**
2 tablespoons	**pine nuts**

Place the soy cream cheese and cherries in a bowl. Mix well. Divide the mixture between the center of the pear halves and press the pear halves back together.

Mix the melted margarine, syrup, and pine nuts and put on a plate. Roll the pears in the nut mixture and place in serving dishes. Refrigerate 1 hour.

Papaya with Bean Curd

Serves 2

4	carrots, grated
Juice of 1	lemon
¼ teaspoon	ground cloves
2 teaspoons	cinnamon
2 teaspoons	raw cane sugar
1	papaya, halved and seeded
½ cup	sweet red bean curd paste

Preheat oven to 350°F.

In a skillet, combine and cook the carrots, lemon juice, spices, and sugar. Spoon into the papaya halves then nestle the bean curd paste in the center of the carrots. Cover the papayas with aluminium foil and bake 15 minutes until the papaya is very soft and bean curd warm.

Garnish with lemon wedge and cherry if desired.

Pears in Lemon Syrup

Serves 8

3 tablespoons	karo syrup
3 tablespoons	raw sugar
1 sprig	fresh rosemary
Juice of 1	lemon
½ cup	organic white wine
¼ cup	water
4	firm bosc pears, peeled and cut into wedges

In a saucepan, combine the syrup and sugar; cook 3 minutes. Add the rosemary and lemon juice; cook 1 minute. Now add the wine and water; simmer for 3 minutes.

Add the pears and cook 8–15 minutes until tender. Remove the pears. Simmer the syrup for 4–5 minutes until it thickens. Cool slightly then return the pears to the pan and reheat them.

Great served over Polenta Pound Cake (page 239).

Strawberry Short Biscuits

Serves 10

Biscuits:

1¼ cup	whole-wheat flour
½ tablespoon	baking powder
¼ teaspoon	sea salt
¼ cup	melted Smart Balance spread
½ cup	oat milk
1 teaspoon	maple syrup

Topping:

2 pints	strawberries, trimmed and sliced (except for 10 berries)
3 teaspoons	maple syrup
3 tablespoons	sweet Gewurztraminer wine
	non-dairy whipped topping

Preheat the oven to 425°F.

Combine all the biscuit ingredients to form a dough. Flour a work surface and roll out the dough to 1-inch thickness. Cut out biscuits using a cutter or jelly jar and place on an oil-sprayed cookie sheet. Bake 25–30 minutes or until brown; cool.

Combine the strawberries, syrup, and wine. Refrigerate for at least one hour. Cut in the biscuits in half, spoon the strawberries onto the biscuits, mound with 1–3 tablespoons non-dairy topping, place other half biscuit on top, and garnish with dab of non-dairy topping and a whole strawberry.

Turt's Fondue

Serves 4 plus

12	Turtles (see Turtles Rule recipe page 248)
¼ cup	non-dairy whipped topping
¼ teaspoon	allspice
	Slices of strawberries, bananas, kiwifruit, oranges, pineapples

Chop up the turtles and place in double boiler. Add the topping and allspice; stir until melted. Serve with the fruit for dipping.

Bread Pudding

Serves 6

3½ cups	multigrain milk
¾ cup	hickory syrup
1	vanilla bean, split and scraped
1 teaspoon	cinnamon
½ teaspoon	salt
4 cups	stale bread, cubed

Preheat the oven to 325°F.

Combine the milk, syrup, vanilla, cinnamon, and salt. Pour the mixture over the bread cubes. Place in an oiled 9-inch baking pan and bake until set and lightly browned, 15–20 minutes.

Chai Tiramisu Blackberry Parfait

Serves 8

64	non-dairy vanilla wafers, crumbled
½ cup	strong Chai green tea
16 ounces	soy cream cheese
4 tablespoons	powdered sugar
1 teaspoon	vanilla extract
2 cups	non-dairy whipped topping
1½ cups	fresh blackberries
3 teaspoons	organic blackberry liqueur

Place the wafers in a bowl and drizzle with the tea. Beat the soy cream cheese, powdered sugar, and vanilla until very smooth. Fold in 1½ cups of the whipped topping. Rinse the blackberries, drain well, and combine with the liqueur.

Layer the various mixtures in tall parfait glasses: Wafers, "cheese," and blackberries. Repeat. Refrigerate at least one hour. Top each parfait with a dollop of the remaining whipped topping and a couple blackberries.

Hickory Tofruity Dessert

Serves 6

12 ounces	soy cream cheese
1 cup	hickory syrup plus 2 tablespoons
6	hazelnut cradles or 12 Veganaise cookies
2 cups	raspberries, strawberries or boysenberries, washed
¼ cup	candied hazelnuts

Mix the soy cream cheese and 1 cup syrup. Fill each cradle with the mixture or mound it on the tops of the Veganaise cookies. Follow with a topping of berries, drizzle with the remaining syrup and sprinkle with candied nuts. If using a cookie, top to the side.

Kahlúa Mousse

Serves 8

1¼ cups	carob chips
½ teaspoon	instant coffee
½ cup	Kahlúa liqueur
16 ounces	non-dairy whipped topping
	coffee beans

In a double boiler, mix the chips, coffee, and liqueur; melt, stirring for about 4 minutes.

Allow it to cool then fold in the topping. Spoon into dishes and garnish with a crushed coffee bean. Refrigerate 1 hour or overnight.

Mardi Gras Bread Pudding

Serves 8–12

2 cups	oat milk
½ cup	brown sugar
1 teaspoon	vanilla extract
½ teaspoon	nutmeg
1 teaspoon	cinnamon
4 tablespoons	egg replacer
2 cups	cranberry sauce
½ cup	pecans, chopped
2 cups	cubed French bread
¾ cup	carob chips
	powdered sugar, carob chips, whipped topping, and pecans to garnish

Preheat the oven to 350°F.

Combine the first six ingredients in a saucepan. Once mixed, add the cranberry sauce and pecans.

Place the bread cubes in a large mixing bowl, add the cranberry mixture and stir together, being certain to coat all the cubes very well. Pat down and allow to soak for 30 minutes.

Oil a bread or cake pan, pour bread mixture into the pan and top with the carob chips. Bake for 50–60 minutes.

Invert the pudding and cut into slices. Garnish with powdered sugar, carob chips, whipped topping (if desired, add 2 teaspoons bourbon to topping) and a few pecans.

Throw me some beads, please!

Old-Fashioned Rice Pudd'n and "Bugs"

Serves 12 plus

2 cups	short-grain rice, cooked
8 cups	multigrain milk
2 cups	cane sugar
2 teaspoons	cinnamon
1 teaspoon	nutmeg
1	vanilla bean, split and scraped
½ cup	cornstarch mixed in 1 cup cold water
¾ cup	raisins

Mix all the ingredients, except the cornstarch and raisins, in a large pot and bring to a boil. Add the cornstarch and stir constantly until thickened. Add the raisins. Cool 45 minutes and serve at room temperature.

For a Tropical Rice Pudding, add ½ cup flaked coconut and 1 cup crushed pineapple instead of raisins.

Punkin's Mousse 2003

Serves 6

12 ounces	tofu
½ cup	hickory syrup
1 teaspoon	lime zest
¼ cup	lemon juice
2 teaspoons	vanilla extract
1 teaspoon	cinnamon
¼ teaspoon	cloves
3 cups	cooked, mashed pumpkin
6	vegan vanilla wafers, crushed

Place all the ingredients, except the pumpkin and vanilla wafers, in a food processor and process. Slowly add pumpkin until creamy. Refrigerate overnight. Spoon the mixture into parfait glasses and garnish with the wafer crumbs.

Add a Punkin feather and you'll be the talk of the town!

Cocoa Banana Sorbet

Yields 1 quart

2 cups	water
¾ cup	raw sugar
1	large ripe banana
4 tablespoons	cocoa powder
1 cup	light corn syrup

Bring the water and sugar to a boil in a saucepan. Set aside to cool.

Mash the banana and add the cocoa powder. Add the sugar syrup and corn syrup. Refrigerate until cold.

Pour the chilled sorbet base into an ice cream maker and process according to manufacturer's instructions. Store in the freezer.

Great served with Pomegranate Sauce (page 346).

Hint-of-Lavender Mango Bliss Sorbet

Serves 4

1	mango, peeled and pitted*
1½ cups	water
1 tablespoon	dried lavender flowers
¾ cup	light corn syrup
	candied lavender flowers for garnish

Puree the mango. Bring the water and syrup to a boil in a saucepan. Cool. Add the lavender and allow to rest for 30 minutes. Add the pureed mango and again bring to a boil. Cool.

Transfer to a sorbet maker and prepare according to manufacturer's directions.

Freeze for at least 8 hours. Garnish with the lavender flowers.

* As an alternative, why not make Pear, Peach or Blueberry Sorbet. Simply omit the mango and lavender and substitute either 2 seeded pears, 2 pitted peaches, or 2 cups of blueberries.

Kiwi Sherbet

Yields 1 quart

1 cup	**water**
1 cup	**raw sugar**
8	**kiwifruit, peeled**
½ cup	**lemon juice**

Bring the water and sugar to a boil in a saucepan. Set aside to cool.

Place the kiwifruit in a blender and puree. Add the sugar syrup and lemon juice. Refrigerate until cold.

Pour the chilled sherbet base into an ice cream maker and process according to manufacturer's instructions. Store in the freezer.

Great served with slices of kiwifruit and lemon zest.

Lemon and Lime
Granita ... Gotcha!

Serves 4

¾ cup	water
¾ cup	raw sugar
3 tablespoons	fresh mint
1 cup	lemon juice
1 cup	limejuice

Bring the water, sugar, and mint to a boil in a saucepan. Stir to help dissolve the sugar. Remove the mint and set aside to cool.

Stir the syrup into the juices. Pour the mixture into a container and freeze. Stir occasionally with a fork, every hour or so, for about 6 hours (the granita will become granular).

Scrape up and serve as a palate cleanser between courses, an aperitif, or a refreshing dessert.

Lemon Twist Sorbet

Serves 8

1¼ cups	raw sugar
¼ cup	light corn syrup
2 tablespoons	chopped fresh rosemary
7	large lemons (about 1½ cups juice)
2 teaspoons	lemon zest
	rosemary sprigs for garnish

In 2-quart saucepan, heat 1½ cups water, the sugar, and syrup; dissolve and bring to a boil. Remove from the heat and stir in the rosemary. Cover and let sit 30 minutes.

Strain the liquid. Add the lemon juice and zest. Pour into a sorbet maker and proceed according to the manufacturer's instructions. Freeze.

Garnish with rosemary sprigs.

Pina Colada Sorbet

Yields 1 quart

1 cup	water
1 cup	raw sugar
1 cup	corn syrup
1 cup	fresh pineapple juice
4 tablespoons	fresh grated coconut

Bring the water and sugar to a boil in a saucepan. Set aside to cool. Add the cooled sugar syrup to the corn syrup, pineapple juice, and coconut. Refrigerate until cold.

Pour the chilled sorbet base into an ice cream maker and process according to the manufacturer's instructions. Store in the freezer.

Great served with Spiced Rum Sauce (page 347).

Splendid Sorbet Mold

Serves 12 slices

1 quantity	**each Pear Sorbet and Blueberry Sorbet (see alternative under Hint-of-Lavender Mango Sorbet 292)**
½ quantity	**Vanilla Carob Glace recipe (page 299)** **your favorite Jello mold**

Make and freeze the sorbets at least one day in advance. Freeze the mold at least a day ahead also.

One hour before putting it all together, place the sorbets in refrigerator to soften. Take the mold out, put a layer of pear sorbet in bottom of the mold and up the sides. Freeze for one day. Repeat with the blueberry sorbet. Freeze for another day. Finish with the Vanilla Bean Glace and smooth the top. Cover with plastic wrap and freeze one more time. Serve within 48 hours.

Unmold by placing warm towels over mold or, if available, heating the mold using a butane torch. Garnish with pear slices and blueberries (or peach slices or blueberries).

Tamarind Sorbet

Yields 1 quart

2 cups	water
1 cup	raw sugar
12 ounces	tamarind pods
1 cup	corn syrup

Bring the water and sugar to a boil in a saucepan. Set aside to cool. Place the tamarind pods in 1 cup of water and boil. Strain through a colander and retrieve 1 cup of pulp. Add the sugar syrup and corn syrup to the pulp and refrigerate until cold.

Pour the chilled sorbet into an ice cream maker and process according to manufacturer's instructions. Store in the freezer.

Tangerine Glace

Serves 8

2 cups	plain soy yogurt
½ cup	corn syrup
2 cups	tangerine sections, puréed
½ cup	tangerine juice

Combine all the ingredients and bring to a boil in a saucepan. Allow to cool. Pour the glace into an ice cream maker and process according to manufacturer's instructions. Store in the freezer.

Vanilla Carob Glace

Yields 2 cups

2 cups	vanilla almond milk
1	vanilla bean
2 cups	cane sugar
Pinch of	salt
3 tablespoons	egg replacer
1 cup	white carob chips

Heat the milk and vanilla bean in a saucepan. Add the sugar and stir until dissolved. Remove from heat and discard the bean. Add the salt and egg replacer; mix well. Blend in the carob chips and set aside to cool.

Place in ice cream/sorbet machine and process according to manufacturer's instructions.

Pantry Essentials:

SAUCES, SALSAS,

GRAVIES, DIPS, DRESSINGS,

CHUTNEYS, MARINADES...

THE FUNDAMENTAL STUFF!

These are the little recipes that mold
your dishes into a flavorful fusion ...
sort of vegan food feng shui

Cucumber Dressing

Yields 2 cups

1	cucumber, peeled and chopped
1 cup	tahini paste
2 tablespoons	tamari
1	garlic clove, minced
¼ cup	white wine vinegar
1 tablespoon	chopped fresh dill
Dash of	pepper

Combine all the ingredients in a blender and puree until silky smooth.

Refrigerate.

Guacamole "Dressing"

Yields 2 cups

2	ripe haas avocados
2	scallions, chopped
¼ cup	oat milk
1 cup	veggie sour cream
1 teaspoon	powered vegetable seasoning
1 tablespoon	tamari sauce
½ teaspoon	red-pepper flakes
½ teaspoon	minced garlic
2 teaspoons	finely diced green bell pepper
1	small tomato, diced

Place all the ingredients, except the bell pepper and tomato, in a blender. Blend until smooth. Mix in the diced bell pepper and tomato. Refrigerate 2–3 hours. Serve with veggie tacos, chips, etc.

Million Island Dressing

Yields 1½ cups

1 cup	vegan mayonnaise dressing
½ cup	Veg-Up (page 319)
½ teaspoon	minced onion
¼ teaspoon	sea salt
1	garlic clove, minced
3 teaspoons	sweet pickle relish
1 teaspoon	pimento
1 teaspoon	chopped kalamata olive

Mix all the ingredients together. Where's Ed with that check?

Pacifica Dressing

Yields 1½ cups

1 teaspoon	olive oil
3	shallots, finely chopped
1 teaspoon	brown mustard
3 tablespoons	wine vinegar
1 tablespoon	fresh tarragon
1 tablespoon	chopped fresh parsley
1 teaspoon	sea salt
1½ cups	vegan mayonnaise

Heat the oil in a saucepan. Sauté the shallot, then add the mustard and vinegar; heat to reduce to 1½ tablespoons. Mix in the rest of ingredients and add vinegar. Remove from the pan and chill.

Serve with Veggie Lobster Tarra-gone (page 184).

Ranch Dressing

Yields 1 cup

½ cup	silken tofu
¼ cup	apple cider vinegar
2	garlic cloves, minced
2 tablespoons	olive oil
2 tablespoons	minced fresh flat-leaf parsley
1 teaspoon	Dijon mustard
1 teaspoon	maple syrup
½ teaspoon	fresh oregano
¼ teaspoon	fresh thyme
	salt and pepper to taste
	oat milk as needed

Put all the ingredients in a blender and blend thoroughly.
Refrigerate for up to one week.

Sesame Dressing

Yields 1 cup

½ cup	sesame oil
1 tablespoons	sesame seeds, toasted
4 tablespoons	minced onion
2	garlic cloves, minced
½ cup	rice vinegar
4 tablespoons	tamari
¼ cup	white corn syrup
	pepper to taste

Heat 1 teaspoon of the oil in a skillet. Add the sesame seeds and heat until toasted, about 2 minutes.

Sauté the onion and garlic in the oil for about 2 minutes. Place the rest of the oil, the vinegar, tamari, and syrup in a screw-top bottle. Add garlic, onion, sesame seeds, and pepper. Shake until mixed.

Tangy Herb Dressing

Yields 3 cups

2 cups	safflower oil
¾ cup	lemon juice
3	garlic cloves, minced
½ teaspoon	sea salt
1 teaspoon	fresh basil
1 teaspoon	fresh thyme
1 teaspoon	fresh sage
1 teaspoon	fresh tarragon
1 teaspoon	fresh marjoram
1 tablespoon	fresh parsley
2 tablespoons	hickory shagbark syrup
3 tablespoons	diced tomatoes

Combine all the ingredients in a screw-top bottle and shake well.

"Taste of Honey" Mustard Dressing

Yields 2 cups

1 cup	olive oil
1	garlic clove, minced
¼ cup	spicy brown mustard
½ cup	corn syrup
½ cup	balsamic vinegar

Heat the oil in a skillet, add the garlic, and fry. Remove garlic and reduce heat to low. Add the mustard and syrup and mix until very smooth. Add vinegar and whisk into dressing. Remove from the heat and mix with your favorite greens.

Blood Orange Sauce
for Veggies

Yields 1 cup

2 tablespoons	egg replacer
1 tablespoon	hot water
8 ounces	vegetable margarine
¼ cup	blood orange juice
Pinch of	salt and cayenne

Whip the egg replacer and water in a saucepan, over low heat; slowly add the margarine continuing to stir and heat gently

Add the orange juice and continue stirring until the juice is reduced to 2 tablespoons; season to taste.

Serve over Brussels sprouts or asparagus.

Don's Orange Sauce

Yields 2 cups

2 cups	orange juice
Juice from 1	lime
1 teaspoon	Triple Sec
1 tablespoon	lemon zest
4 tablespoons	arrowroot

Reserve 4 tablespoons of the orange juice. Place the remaining orange juice in a saucepan with the limejuice. Bring to a boil and add the zest.

Mix the reserved four tablespoons juice with the arrowroot; add to pan and stir, allowing it to thicken. Reduce the heat. Add the Triple Sec and simmer an additional 2 minutes.

Great with spring rolls.

Faux Béchamel Sauce

Yields 3 cups

3 cups	multigrain milk
3 tablespoons	vegetable margarine
3 tablespoons	flour
¼ teaspoon	nutmeg

Heat the milk in a saucepan, over a medium heat, until it begins to steam. Place the margarine in another pan and melt. Slowly mix the flour into the margarine until it becomes a roux, or paste. Mix the nutmeg with the milk and then, little by little, add the milk to the margarine, stirring constantly until thickened, about 5 minutes.

Use in lasagna, moussaka, and pasta dishes calling for béchamel sauce.

Garlic Dipping Sauce (Fondue)

Yields 1 cup

⅓ cup	vegetable broth + ¼ cup
⅓ cup	sherry
4	scallions, thinly sliced
1 head	garlic, cloves slivered
4 teaspoons	tamari
3 tablespoons	limejuice
3 teaspoons	maple syrup
1 tablespoon	minced ginger root
1 teaspoon	cornstarch

Combine all the ingredients, except the ¼ cup of vegetable broth and cornstarch, in a saucepan and bring to a boil. Reduce the heat and mix the remaining broth with the cornstarch. Stir into the pan, allow to thicken, and serve.

Hickory Orange Chili Sauce

Yields 1 plus cups

1 cup	hickory syrup
¼ cup	apple cider vinegar
3 tablespoons	orange zest
2 tablespoons	chopped fresh oregano
1½ teaspoons	ancho chili powder
2	garlic cloves, minced
Dash of	salt

Place all the ingredients in a saucepan and bring to a boil. Allow to cool.

Use as marinade for tofu, veggie chicken, toast-tip dip, or salad dressing.

La Costa
Sweet 'n' Sour Sauce

Yields 2 cups

1 cup	rice vinegar
½ cup	fresh apple juice
½ cup	fresh carrot juice
¼ cup	light Karo syrup
Dash of	Tabasco
2 teaspoons	white pepper
4 tablespoons	cornstarch

Mix all the liquid ingredients and the pepper in a saucepan over low heat. If you wish to serve this as a sauce (as opposed to using it as a marinade), thicken it with the cornstarch mixed with a little water. For a marinade, leave out the cornstarch.

To give the sauce a bit of texture you can add ¼ cup grated carrot and 1 grated apple.

Picnic Barbecue Sauce

Yields 3 cups

1 tablespoon	olive oil
4 tablespoons	minced onion
3	garlic cloves, minced
½ cup	chopped cilantro
	Liquid Smoke, any favorite flavor
15	medium tomatoes, peeled
¼ cup	limejuice
½ cup	maple syrup
½ cup	corn syrup
6 tablespoons	tamari
¼ cup	white vinegar

Place the oil, onion, garlic, and cilantro in a small skillet; sauté 2 minutes. During the last 30 seconds add 2 dashes of liquid smoke. Remove from the heat.

Place the rest of the ingredients in a blender and puree. Add the sautéed mixture and combine well. Serve over Casa de Granada Hills "Chicken" Breasts (page 119) etc.

Rancheros Sauce

Yields 4 cups

8 ounces	chopped green chilies
	safflower oil
2	garlic cloves
2	onions, minced
1 teaspoon	minced cilantro
4 cups	fresh tomatoes, seeded, peeled, and chopped
Juice of 1	orange

Rinse the chilies and sauté in the safflower oil, along with the garlic and onion. Add the rest of the ingredients and cook 5 minutes. Pour over enchiladas.

Red Sauce ... for Pasta

Yields 3 cups

4 teaspoons	olive oil
1 teaspoon	fresh rosemary
¼ cup	chopped onion
4	garlic cloves, minced
4 cups	tomatoes, diced
¼ cup	chopped fresh basil
¼ cup	diced black olives or 2 tablespoons capers
1 cup	Cabernet Sauvignon
	salt and pepper

Heat the olive oil in a skillet. Add the rosemary, onion, and garlic; sauté. Add the tomatoes and basil; simmer 15 minutes. Remove from the heat and puree in food processor.

Return to the heat, add the olives or capers, and, as the sauce comes to a boil, the wine. Reduce the heat and simmer 10 minutes more. Adjust seasoning as desired.

Serve over pasta.

Soy Yogurt Tahini Sauce

Yields 1½ cups

1 cup	soy yogurt
½ cup	tahini paste
1 tablespoon	olive oil
Juice of 1	lemon
	Salt and pepper to taste

Blend all the ingredients together and refrigerate overnight.

Serve with Indian or Mediterranean dishes.

Sweet Miso Sauce

Yields 1 cup

½ cup	white or yellow miso
¼ cup	hickory shagbark syrup
¼ cup	rice vinegar
¼ cup	sesame oil
3 tablespoons	toasted sesame seeds
2	jalapeño peppers, minced
½ teaspoon	grated ginger root
2 teaspoons	tamari

Mix all ingredients together in blender. Place in a saucepan and simmer 2 minutes.

Serve warm.

White Sauce...
for Pasta

Yields 3 cups

2 teaspoons	olive oil
2 tablespoons	marjoram
2 teaspoons	savory
¼ cup	chopped white onion
Juice of 1	lemon
3	garlic cloves, minced
1 cup	white wine
6 ounces	soy cream cheese
4 cups	almond milk
½ teaspoon	nutmeg
	salt and pepper

Heat the oil in a skillet with the marjoram and savory. Add the onion, lemon juice, and garlic; sauté. Deglaze with the wine.

Beat the soy cream cheese with the milk. Add the nutmeg. Place in a saucepan and add the onion mixture. Simmer until the sauce thickens; season to taste.

Serve over pasta and garnish with veggie parmesan cheese.

Veg-Up!

Yields 2 cups

6	tomatoes
1	beet
12	carrots
6	celery ribs
1 head	romaine lettuce
1 bunch	fresh parsley
1 handful	fresh cilantro
1 bunch	spinach
1 cup	white vinegar
4 teaspoons	sea salt
1 can (8oz)	tomato paste

Juice all the vegetables and herbs. Place in a saucepan and add the vinegar, sea salt, and tomato paste. Simmer until thickened, 10 minutes or so. Adjust seasoning and, if you wish, add ½ teaspoon black pepper. Cool then place in a jar. Keeps one week in the refrigerator. Serve as condiment on veggie burgers, with potatoes, etc.

Wasabi Sauce

Yields 1 cup

1 cup	vegan mayonnaise dressing
4 teaspoons	tamari
1 teaspoon	lemon zest
2 teaspoons	wasabi paste
2 teaspoons	cane syrup

Whip all the ingredients together. Ohm!

Savory Gravy

Yields 2 cups

16 ounces	firm tofu
¾ cup	vegetable broth
¼ cup + 2 tablespoons	tamari
¾ cup	corn oil
2 tablespoons	brewers yeast flakes
2 teaspoons	sunflower seeds
2	garlic cloves
Juice of 1	lemon*
½ teaspoon	kelp powder
2 tablespoons	fresh basil or sage
½ teaspoon	powdered vegetable seasoning
1 tablespoon	chopped fresh chives

Place all the ingredients in a blender and puree until smooth. Use as topping on everything—pasta, vegetables, tofu, tempeh, as a cheese or salad dressing etc. It's especially good served warm. It also freezes well.

* If using this as an enchilada sauce, substitute a lime for the lemon.

World's Best Veggie Gravy

Yields 5 cups

4¼ cups	water or vegetable broth
¼ cup	very finely diced celery
2 tablespoons	minced white onion
½ cup	brown mushrooms, sliced
1	garlic clove, minced
¼ teaspoon	paprika
½ teaspoon	white pepper
4 tablespoons	tamari
3 tablespoons	cornstarch

Place all the ingredients, except the cornstarch, in saucepan and bring to a boil, about 8 minutes. Remove ¼ cup broth from the pan, allow to cool then mix with the cornstarch. Slowly stir the mixture into the pan and place over a medium heat until the gravy thickens, about 10 minutes.

For variety, try adding ¼ cup of chopped walnuts. To make a creamy, country-type gravy, substitute soymilk for the water.

Green Chutney

Yields 1 cup

1 cup	**cilantro leaves, chopped**
2	**green chilies, roasted, seeded, and chopped**
½ tablespoon	**grated ginger root**
3 tablespoons	**lemon juice**
Pinch of	**sea salt and cracked black pepper**

Place the cilantro, chilies, and ginger in a food processor; mix. Add the lemon juice and season to taste. If the paste is too thick, add water to desired consistency.

Serve with your favorite Indian dishes.

Minty Mango Chutney

Yields 2 cups

¼	red onion, diced very small
1 tablespoon	white wine vinegar
Juice and pulp of 4	limes
¼ cup	corn syrup
¼ teaspoon	cinnamon
¼ teaspoon	cayenne pepper
1 bunch	fresh mint, chopped
2	mangoes, peeled and flesh cut into ½-inch pieces

Boil the water in a pan and add the onion. Remove after 1 minute and toss the onion with the vinegar. Reserve. In a saucepan, combine the lime, syrup, spices, and mint. Cook over medium heat for 3 minutes until thickened. Mix the mango with the onions. Add the syrup and stir. Let the chutney rest at room temperature for 1 hour then serve.

Tamarind Chutney

Yields 2 cups

½ pound	tamarind
3 cups	water
½ teaspoon	sea salt
½ teaspoon	cumin
1	tomato, finely chopped
½ cup	raw sugar
½ teaspoon	chili powder
1 tablespoon	cider vinegar

Soak the tamarind overnight in water. Remove the seeds, place in a blender and puree. Place in a saucepan and add salt, cumin, tomatoes, and sugar; bring to a boil. Reduce the heat and mix in the chili powder and vinegar.

Serve as a condiment with curry.

Holiday Cranberry Relish

Yields about 4 cups

1 pound	**fresh cranberries**
½ cup	**maple syrup**
½ cup	**freshly squeezed orange juice, pulp and all**
2	**pears, finely diced**
1 teaspoon	**grated lemon peel**
4 tablespoons	**port**

Place the cranberries, syrup, and orange juice in a saucepan and bring to a slow boil, about 6 minutes. Add the pears and grated lemon peel; simmer 2 minutes. Add the port, mix thoroughly and serve.

Serve as relish with winter squash or veggie turkey.

Quick Orange Marmalade

Yields 4 cups

6	**large oranges, sliced and diced**
1	**lemon, sliced and diced**
2 cups	**karo syrup**
2	**cloves, ground**
½ cup	**port**

Mix all the ingredients in a saucepan and bring to a boil, stirring constantly. Simmer until the mixture is thick and the peels are caramelized, about 20 minutes. Turn into a dish and refrigerate.

Celery Salsa

Yields 1 cup

4	celery ribs, diced
½ cup	diced red onion
½ cup	thinly sliced scallions
1	jalapeño pepper, roasted, seeds removed, and diced
½ teaspoon	salt
1 teaspoon	lime zest
Juice of 1	lime
1 teaspoon	maple syrup
1	banana, diced

Combine all the ingredients, folding in the banana last.

Great with veggie salmon, melba toasts, etc.

Fresco Salsa

Yields 2 cups

1	medium yellow crookneck squash, shredded
1	small zucchini, diced
½ cup	fresh corn
4 tablespoons	limejuice
6	medium tomatoes, diced
2 tablespoons	red onion, diced
1	jalapeño pepper, seeded and diced finely
2	garlic cloves, minced

Spread the squash and corn on aluminum foil and roast 7 minutes over a barbecue, basting with 2 tablespoons of the limejuice. Cool.

Mix all the ingredients together and refrigerate for 48 hours. Bring to room temperature before serving.

Haute Mango Salsa

Yields 2 cups

1 tablespoon	olive oil
6 tablespoons	minced onion
2	garlic cloves, minced
2	celery ribs, diced
1 teaspoon	peppercorns
1	serrano chili, seeded and peeled
¼ cup	lemon juice
3 teaspoons	grated lemon peel
6 tablespoons	organic white wine
3	mangoes, pureed
	sea salt

Place oil in a skillet, add the onion, garlic, celery, peppercorns, and chili; sauté. Add lemon juice, peel, and wine. Cool.

Add the cooled mixture to the mango puree and puree once again. Season with salt and refrigerate.

Pineapple Papaya Salsa

Yields 2 cups

1	ripe papaya, peeled
1 cup	crushed pineapple
Juice of 1	lemon
1 teaspoon	sambal
¼ cup	corn oil
	salt and pepper

In blender, mix the papaya, pineapple, lemon juice, and sambal.

Add the oil slowly, and season to taste.

Red Salsa

Yields 1 quart

1	yellow onion, sliced thin
2 tablespoons	olive oil
14	roma tomatoes, diced
2	garlic cloves, minced
1 cup	celery juice
1	jalapeño chili, stemmed and seeded
1 teaspoon	sea salt
6 tablespoons	tamari

Sauté the onions in the oil for 10 minutes. Place all the ingredients in a blender and puree.

Place the puree in a saucepan and bring to a boil; reduce heat and simmer 20 minutes. Refrigerate.

Strawberry Salsa

Yields 3 cups

2 cups	ripe strawberries, chopped
1 cup	ripe tomatoes, diced
½ cup	red onion, minced
¼ cup	fresh mint, chopped
2 tablespoons	chopped fresh cilantro
2	jalapeño peppers, minced (seeds removed)
1 teaspoon	lime and lemon zest
1 tablespoon	each lime and lemon juice
1 tablespoon	balsamic vinegar
	salt and pepper to taste

Mix all the ingredients and chill overnight.

Tomatillo Salsa

Yields 2 cups

1 pound	tomatillos, husks removed
3	jalapeño peppers, seeded
¼ cup	chopped white onion
Juice of 1	lime
2 tablespoons	chopped fresh cilantro
½ cup	chopped orange bell pepper
¼ teaspoon	sea salt
¼ teaspoon	red-pepper flakes
½ teaspoon	corn syrup
Splash of	garlic vinegar

In a blender, mix three-quarters of the tomatillos and all the remaining ingredients (except syrup and vinegar) until they form a coarse puree.

Dice the remaining tomatillos and blend into the mixture along with a slash of vinegar and the syrup. Allow to rest at room temperature one hour before serving.

Serve with veggie tacos, scrambled tofu, Chili Relleno Brunchfast (page 357) etc.

Bean Dip

Yields 1 cup

1 cup	cannellini beans, cooked and drained
3	garlic cloves, minced
Juice of 1	lemon
Pinch of	salt and pepper
1 teaspoon	fresh oregano
	extra virgin olive oil
	fresh parsley or cilantro to garnish

Place all the ingredients, except the oil and garnish, in a food processor; puree. Add the oil little by little to desired consistency. Adjust seasoning to taste. Garnish with parsley or cilantro.

Great with veggies, pita bread—you name it!

Beggar's Caviar

Serves 4

1	eggplant
2 teaspoons	sea salt
4 tablespoons	Veg-Up (page 319)
1 teaspoon	black pepper
3 teaspoons	lemon juice
3	garlic cloves, minced
1 teaspoon	maple syrup
3 teaspoons	tahini paste
4 teaspoons	chopped fresh parsley
	wheat pita chip triangles to serve

Cut the eggplant in half. Salt it, leave to stand then press out the excess moisture. Baste with Veg-Up and place in an oven or barbecue and roast until tender, 30 minutes or so. Cool and place in a freezer bag. Snip a hole in the corner of the bag and squeeze the eggplant into a bowl. Mix with the rest of the ingredients and serve with the pita chip triangles.

Carrot Salad Spread

Yields 1 cup

10	carrots
⅔ cup	tahini paste
2 tablespoons	white miso
½ teaspoon	celery seed
2	garlic cloves, minced
2 tablespoons	sunflower seeds
1 tablespoon	dried currants
Dash of	cayenne pepper

Juice the carrots. Process the tahini and miso then add the carrot juice. Now blend in rest of the ingredients.

Serve on melba toasts, pita chip triangles, or root rounds.

Garlic Spread

Yields 1 cup

40	garlic cloves (peeled)
3 cups	olive oil

Place the garlic in a skillet and cover with the oil. Cover with a lid and cook on low for 20 minutes. Drain the oil and place the garlic on a rack to drain.

Serve the warm cloves with warm French bread.

Hickory Apple "Butter"

Yields 1 cup

3	large granny smith apples, cored and quartered
1	shallot, minced
¼ cup	hickory syrup
1 teaspoon	cloves
½ teaspoon	cinnamon
¼ teaspoon	dry mustard
	salt and pepper to taste

Put the apples and shallot in saucepan, cover with water and cook until soft. Drain the apples and shallots, add the remaining ingredients and puree.

Use as spread for crackers and veggies.

Hickory Pistachio Pesto

Yields 2 cups

4 tablespoons	hickory syrup
1 cup	roasted pistachios
6	garlic cloves
¾ cup	veggie Parmesan
½ cup	fresh parsley
½ cup	fresh basil
2 teaspoons	balsamic vinegar
6 tablespoons	olive oil
	salt and pepper to taste
	truffle oil to garnish

Process all the ingredients. Garnish with truffle oil.

Serve over pasta, with garlic toast, etc.

Olive Tapenade

Yields 2 cups

1 cup	olive oil
1 cup	mushrooms, diced
3	garlic cloves, chopped
1 cup	black olives, diced
½ tablespoon	cracked black pepper
1 tablespoon	pimentos

Heat the oil in a skillet, add the mushrooms, and sauté.
Remove from the heat and add the remaining ingredients.
Refrigerate overnight. Serve on bread slices as a relish.

Roasted Red Pepper Hummus Dip

Yields 2 cups

2 cups	chickpeas, rinsed very well
4 tablespoons	sea salt
2 cups	water
3	garlic cloves, minced
1	red bell pepper, washed and seeded
10 ounces	silken tofu
1 teaspoon	white pepper
1 teaspoon	red-pepper flakes
4 teaspoons	lemon juice

Place the chickpeas in a pan, add the sea salt, and water; cook until tender, about 1½ hours. Drain. Mix the garlic with the red bell pepper and roast under broiler for 5 minutes. Place all the ingredients in blender and puree. Refrigerate.

Serve with pita bread or crackers as a dip or spread.

Simple Aioli

Yields 1 cup

5	garlic cloves
1 cup + 4 tablespoons	extra virgin olive oil
1 teaspoon	mustard
¼ teaspoon	salt
¼ teaspoon	white pepper
Juice of ½	lemon

Sauté the garlic cloves in the 4 tablespoons of olive oil and cool. Mince the garlic in a small food processor then slowly add the remaining oil, very little at a time, adding more as it thickens. Once the oil has been incorporated, add the mustard, salt and pepper, then the lemon juice.

Variations for dips include adding dill, rosemary, tarragon, saffron, five-spice powder or your favorite herb/seasoning.

Smoky Black Bean Hummus

Yields 3 cups

2 cups	cooked black beans
1 tablespoon	hickory syrup
1 teaspoon	liquid smoke
1 cup	chickpeas, cooked
1 tablespoon	minced garlic
1 teaspoon	cumin
2 tablespoons	tahini paste
1 tablespoon	limejuice
2 tablespoons	minced fresh cilantro
¼ cup	olive oil

Place the beans in a saucepan with the syrup and liquid smoke. Cook until the mixture comes to a boil, remove from the heat, and cool. Place all the ingredients in a food processor and puree until smooth. Season with salt and pepper.

Serve with pita chips or veggies.

Snappy Pistachio Spread

Yields about 1½ cups

4 tablespoons	salted pistachio nuts, shelled and roasted (reserve 1 tablespoon for garnish)
2	garlic cloves, roasted and minced
10-ounce package	firm tofu
1 cup	sugar snap peas, shelled and cooked
1½ tablespoons	limejuice
	salt and pepper to taste

Place the pistachios and garlic in the oven at 500° F for 5 minutes, or until browned. Combine all the ingredients in a food processor and blend until smooth. Chop the reserved nuts and sprinkle on top.

Spread on assorted crackers, melba toast, jicama rounds, or celery ribs.

Spinach Dip

Yields 2 cups

2 bunches	spinach, thoroughly rinsed and chopped into 1-inch pieces
1 teaspoon	sea salt
3	garlic cloves, minced
½ teaspoon	turmeric
¼ teaspoon	white pepper
3 tablespoons	lemon juice
2 tablespoons	chopped fresh mint
1 cup	vegan mayonnaise dressing
1 cup	soy cream cheese

Parboil the spinach with the sea salt for 4 minutes. Drain. Process the rest of the ingredients then add the spinach. Refrigerate overnight.

Serve as an appetizer dip with crackers, fresh vegetables etc.

Not Salmon Pate!

Yields 1½ cups

4 ounces	veggie salmon
4 ounces	soy cream cheese
½ cup	vegan mayonnaise dressing
1 teaspoon	lemon juice
1	garlic clove
Pinch of	black pepper
¼ teaspoon	grated ginger root
1 tablespoon	minced red onion
1 tablespoon	chopped fresh chives

In a food processor, mix the veggie salmon, soy cream cheese, veggie mayo, lemon juice, garlic, pepper, and ginger root. Fold in the onion. Garnish with chives.

Vegetable Pate

Yields 1 cup

2 tablespoons	sunflower seeds
2 teaspoons	olive oil
8 ounces	mushrooms, sliced
1 cup	chopped red onion
4	garlic cloves, sliced
1 cup	cooked green lentils
¼ cup	organic Chardonnay
2 tablespoons	tamari
2 tablespoons	pimentos*
½ teaspoon	grated lemon peel

Toast the sunflower seeds in a 425° F oven for 7 minutes. Heat the oil in a skillet and add the mushroom, onion, and garlic; sauté. Add the lentils and wine. Simmer until wine is reduced.

Place mushroom and lentil mixture in a blender and add the remaining ingredients. Puree until smooth. Place in a mold of your choice and refrigerate overnight. If you wish, garnish with lemon and sunflower seeds or green grapes.

Serve as appetizer on crackers, toast, baguette slices, etc.
* You could substitute 2 tablespoons capers for the pimentos for a change.

Herbed Croutons

Serves 8

8 teaspoons	vegetable margarine
8 slices	rye bread, cut into triangles
8 teaspoons	minced fresh parsley
2 tablespoons	minced fresh sage
2 tablespoons	minced fresh thyme
1 tablespoon	minced fresh basil
1 teaspoon	white pepper
Juice of 1	lemon

Grease a lined cookie sheet with the margarine. In plastic bag shake all the remaining ingredients together. Place on the cookie sheet, mix well, and bake in the oven at 275° F for 10 minutes, checking frequently. Once the bread is brown and crisp, cover with foil and turn off oven. Once cooled, place in airtight container or serve with Artichoke Chowder (page 9).

Spicy Soup Croutons

Serves 8

8 slices	whole-wheat bread, cut into triangles
1 teaspoon	each garlic powder, chili powder, and onion powder
2 teaspoons	minced fresh parsley
3 tablespoons	vegetable margarine

Grease a lined cookie sheet with a little margarine. In a plastic bag, shake all the ingredients together then mix well on the cookie sheet. Place in the oven at 275°F for 10 minutes, checking frequently. Once brown and crisp, cover with foil and turn off the oven. Once cooled, place in an airtight container or serve with Split Pea Soup (page 104).

Brandied Cream Sauce

Yields 2 cups

1 cup	apple juice
2 tablespoons	raw sugar
2 tablespoons	arrowroot dissolved in 2 tablespoons apple juice
⅔ cup	vanilla almond milk
4 tablespoons	brandy

Place the apple juice and sugar in a saucepan; bring to a boil. Reduce the heat and add the arrowroot, allowing the sauce to thicken as it simmers. Add the milk and brandy to the apple juice mixture. Cook sauce until heated through and thickened, about 3 minutes. Great with Pumpkin Spice Loaf (page 242).

Pomegranate Sauce

Yields 1½ cups

2 cups	water
¾ cup	raw sugar
2	large pomegranate, peeled and seeds removed
2 teaspoons	lemon juice
½ cup	organic domestic port
½ teaspoon	arrowroot

In a saucepan, bring the water and sugar to a boil. Add the pomegranate seeds and lemon juice, boil again and add the port. Pass the sauce through a colander to remove any remaining seeds. Remove ¼ cup of the liquid and mix in the arrowroot. Return to the saucepan and simmer, stirring gently until thickened.

Soy Cream Cheese Frosting

Yields icing for 1 cake

2½ cups	cane sugar
½ cup	cornstarch
8 ounces	soy cream cheese
1 teaspoon	vanilla extract
1 teaspoon	lemon juice
⅓ cup	vegetable margarine

Mix all the ingredients and whip until smooth. Ice your cake and enjoy!

Spiced Rum Sauce

Yields 1½ cups

1 cup	water
2	cloves
1 cup	raw sugar
8 teaspoons	slivered almonds
¼ cup	dark rum
3 teaspoons	arrowroot

Place the water, cloves, and sugar in a saucepan and bring to a boil. Add the almonds and rum; boil again. Remove the cloves. Reduce the heat, remove 3 teaspoons of the sauce and allow to cool. Mix the cooled sauce with the arrowroot and return to saucepan. Bring to a boil and allow to thicken, stirring constantly. Remove from heat. Cool.

Serve over Pina Colada Sorbet (page 296) or other dessert of your choice.

Candied Flowers

Yields 2 cups

2 tablespoons	rose water
2 tablespoons	powdered gum arabic
2 cups	flowers - rose petals, lavender, violets, pansies (organic of course)
1 cup	fine sugar

Combine the rose water and powered gum. Using a small brush, paint the petals with the mixture and place on a parchment-lined cookie sheet. Liberally sprinkle with sugar. Place another sheet of parchment over the top. Place in the oven on the lowest setting and allow the flowers to dry overnight.

Use as a garnish for sorbets, mousses, and cakes.

Carob Vanilla Filigrees

Yields 4 ounces of your heart's desire!

2 ounces	**carob chips**
2 ounces	**vanilla chips**

Line a cookie sheet with wax paper. Melt the carob chips in a double boiler.

Drizzle onto the cookie sheet into shapes of your choice—leaf, heart ... you name it.
Repeat with the vanilla chips. Place in the refrigerator to harden.

You can also use rose leaves and imprint them onto the candy—simply peel back after they've set.

Use as a garnish with your favorite sorbet, glace, tofu cheesecake etc.

Citrus Peel Candy

Yields ½ cup

4	oranges, lemons, limes, tangerines or grapefruit (or a combination of lemons and limes)
2 cups	water
2½ cups	raw sugar

Peel the rinds off your chosen fruit and cut into long strips. Reserve 1 cup of the juice from your fruit. Place the peel in boiling water and cook for 20 minutes. Drain, reserving the liquid, and rinse. Place the peel back in the pan with the reserved liquid and cook again for 20 minutes. Reserve peel.

In a saucepan, combine the sugar, 1 cup of fruit juice, and the water. Bring to a boil and add the peel. Simmer for 1 hour. Remove the peel and place on a cookie sheet. Sprinkle with raw sugar and allow the peel to dry.

Serve over sorbet, use as topping for favorite desserts, etc.

Naan

Serves 8

2 cups	water
1 package	yeast
Pinch of	sea salt
3 tablespoons	vegetable margarine
½ cup	raw sugar
2 cups	wheat flour

Place water, yeast, and salt in a saucepan with the margarine; mix and heat until warm. Remove from the heat and mix in the sugar and flour. Place on a floured surface and knead three times, resting 10 minutes in between each kneading.

Preheat the oven to 375°F.

Roll out the dough into an oval shape about 1-inch thick. Place on a cookie sheet and bake until brown.

Simple Crêpes

Yields 10 crêpes

½ cup	flour
¼ teaspoon	salt
¾ cup	almond milk
	egg replacer for 3 eggs

Mix the flour and salt. Whisk together the milk and egg replacer. Add the flour and stir until smooth.

Pour the batter, ¼ of a cup at a time, onto a heated (medium) crêpe pan, tilting the pan in all directions so that the batter forms a film over the entire pan. Cook 1–2 minutes until the crêpe will lift easily and is browned on the underside. Turn over and cook an additional 15 seconds. Remove from the heat and cool on waxed paper/paper towels.

Tom's Salty Peas (Nasturtium Pickles)

Yields 2 cups

2 cups	nasturtium seeds (use green seeds)
2 cups	champagne vinegar
¼ cup	sea salt

Combine the ingredients and refrigerate. Use in salads and pasta dishes.

(Tom does not care for capers ... these are a great substitute that he does like!)

Not Egg! Replacer

For 1 egg

2 tablespoons	all-purpose white flour
1½ teaspoons	safflower oil
½ teaspoon	baking powder
2 tablespoons	water

Whisk the ingredients together and use immediately.

'Cottage Cheese'

Serves 4

½ cup	lemon juice
¼ cup	apple cider vinegar
2 cups	oat milk
10 ounces	medium tofu
1 tablespoon	soy oil
2 tablespoons	chopped scallion
1 tablespoon	chopped fresh cilantro
3 teaspoons	tamari

Heat the lemon juice, vinegar, and milk until the curds separate. Strain the curds and mix the tofu with the curds. Place all the ingredients in blender and pulse so that the mixture has some lumps and isn't completely smooth. Add salt to taste.

Serve with fresh fruit, on crackers, etc.

"Cream Cheese"

Serves 8

2 cups	soy yogurt
1 tablespoon	pepper
2 teaspoons	cumin
1 teaspoon	lemon zest
Dash of	red pepper
3 tablespoons	very finely diced red, yellow, orange, and green bell pepper
½ teaspoon	celery seed

Mix all the ingredients. Line a large strainer with a cheesecloth and fold the soy yogurt mixture into the strainer. Wrap up and place in the refrigerator for 24–48 hours.

Serve with fresh veggies or crackers.

Break the Fast:

BREAKFAST PLEASURES—SIMPLE

DISHES TO START YOUR DAY!

The most important meal of
the day should be simple yet
extrvagantly scrumptious!

Apple Pie Waffles

Yields 2 large waffles

½ cup	wheat flake cereal
1 cup	multigrain milk
½ cup	wheat flour
2 tablespoons	baking powder
1 teaspoon	baking soda
½ teaspoon	allspice
¼ teaspoon	salt
½ cup	applesauce
	cinnamon

Soak the wheat flakes in the multigrain milk until soft.

Combine the flour, baking powder, soda, allspice, and salt then add the wheat flakes and applesauce. Pour into an oiled waffle iron and cook until golden. Sprinkle the waffles with some cinnamon to serve.

Great with hickory shagbark syrup.

Chili Rellenos Brunchfast

Serves 6

3 tablespoons	olive oil
2 pounds	soft tofu
2 packages	tofu scrambler
½ cup	multigrain milk
	sea salt and pepper to taste
1 can (8oz)	whole green chilies
4 cups	shredded veggie cheese

Preheat oven to 375°F.

Coat a 9-inch-square ovenproof dish with the olive oil. In a blender, mix the tofu, scrambler, milk, and seasoning. Pour half the mixture into the dish, and add a layer of chilies followed by a layer of veggie cheese. Repeat. Bake for 1 hour, or until done and lightly browned.

Cut into squares and serve with salsa.

Cinnamon Rolls

Serves 8 plus

1 package	vegan freezer dinner rolls or refrigerator biscuits (yeast type)
1 cup	vegan pudding, butterscotch flavor
1 cup	brown sugar
1 cup	cane sugar
1 teaspoon	cinnamon
½ cup	chopped pecans
1 cup	vegetable margarine

Oil a Bundt cake pan and place the rolls on the bottom.

Mix together ½ cup pudding mix and the brown sugar; sprinkle over the rolls. Mix the remaining pudding mix with cane sugar and add the cinnamon; sprinkle over the rolls. Now sprinkle the chopped pecans over the rolls.

Melt the margarine and pour over the rolls. Cover the cake pan, place it in a warm area, and leave for 3 hours to allow it to rise. Bake at 350°F for 35 minutes. Cool upside down and serve warm.

Country-Style Biscuits

Serves 6

3 cups	unbleached white flour
1½ tablespoons	baking powder
1½ tablespoons	cane sugar
½ tablespoon	sea salt
½ cup	vegetable margarine
½ cup	hazelnut milk

Preheat the oven to 425°F.

In large mixing bowl, mix the dry ingredients and sift them together 10 times. Work in the margarine with your hands until the mixture is very fine in texture. Add the milk and mix into a dough, beating it for 1 minute. Drop by the spoonful onto a baking sheet and bake 10 minutes, or until golden brown.

Great with World's Best Gravy (page 321), veggie sausage, and an Ohmlette (page 368).

Don't Hold the Bacon

Yields 30 slices

½ cup	tamari
1 tablespoon	brewer's yeast flakes
1 tablespoon	shagbark syrup
1 teaspoon	hickory liquid smoke
8 ounces	firm tofu

Mix all the ingredients except the tofu. Slice the tofu and marinate 72 hours or more in the marinade. Cook in an oiled griddle until brown and crispy.

Soyrizo Hash

Serves 4

	safflower oil for frying
¼ cup	finely chopped yellow onion
¼ cup	finely chopped red bell pepper
12 ounces	Soyrizo
½ cup	black beans
¾ cup	salsa
½ cup	cornbread crumbs
Dash of	cayenne
	salt and pepper to taste

Heat 4 teaspoons of oil in a skillet, add onion, bell pepper, and Soyrizo; sauté until onions are translucent. Add the beans and salsa; mix well. Add the cornbread crumbs and seasoning. Heat thoroughly.

Great topped with soy sour cream, soy cheese, and more salsa!

Pedro's Hash Brown Short Stacks

Serves 6

Short Stack:

1 cup	soy sour cream
¾ cup	water
3 cups	rye flour
1 teaspoon	baking soda
1½ teaspoons	salt
1½ teaspoons	baking powder
1 tablespoon	caraway seed
3 tablespoons	vegetable margarine
6 ounces	veggie cheddar, shredded

Pedro's Potatoes:

2 pounds	yukon gold potatoes
6 tablespoons	vegetable margarine
2	yellow onions, chopped
½	red and yellow bell pepper, chopped
½ cup	fresh cilantro, minced
	salt and pepper

Preheat oven to 425°F.

Stir sour cream and water together. Mix the dry ingredients then add the margarine a teaspoon at a time. Now mix in the shredded cheese then the sour cream. Blend completely and drop the dough onto greased cookie sheets (6 short stacks). Bake 15–20 minutes, cool slightly, and cut in half.

Peel, cube, and parboil the potatoes. Drain. Heat the margarine in a skillet, add all the ingredients and cook until brown and tender, about 20 minutes. Fill the biscuits. Serve with Red Salsa (page 329) and Tomatillo Salsa (page 331), or Savory Gravy (page 320).

Easy Banana Nut Muffins

Yields 6 jumbo muffins

2 cups	flour
1 teaspoon	baking soda
½ cup	raw sugar
1 teaspoon	each allspice and cinnamon
2	ripe bananas, mashed
1½ cups	almond milk
¼ cup	vegetable margarine, melted
2 tablespoons	egg replacer
¼ cup	chopped walnuts

Preheat the oven to 400°F.

Mix all the dry ingredients, except the egg replacer and nuts, in a medium bowl. Add the banana, milk, and margarine. Mix well—the mixture should be stiff. Add the egg replacer and again mix well. Fold in the nuts.

Oil a muffin pan and place the batter in the pan, filling the cups half way to the top. Sprinkle the tops with raw sugar and cinnamon if you like. Bake 20–25 minutes.

Peachy Strudel

Serves 12

1 cup	dried peaches*
1 tablespoon	balsamic vinegar
1	vanilla bean, split
¼ cup	maple syrup
¼ cup	natural brown cane sugar
½ teaspoon	shredded fresh ginger root
1 cup	water
1 tablespoon	egg replacer
1 cup	pecans, chopped
¼ cup	maple syrup
2 tablespoons	water
6 sheets	phyllo dough
¼ cup	vegetable oil
½ cup	pecans, ground
¼ cup	natural brown sugar

Place the first 6 ingredients in a saucepan and cook over medium heat until syrupy, about 7 minutes. Combine the next 5 ingredients in a separate saucepan and heat until the pecans are lightly browned, about 10 minutes.

Lay out the dough and baste with oil. Sprinkle with some ground pecans and brown sugar. Add the pecan mixture then the peaches, then repeat the dough, pecan, peaches layers two more times. Finish with pecan topping. Roll up and place on cookie sheet.

Bake at 350°F for 10 minutes, or until browned. Cut and serve warm with Vanilla Carob Glace (page 299).
* You can use plums, apples, strawberries, or mangoes for variety!

Flax Seed Hot Cakes

Serves 4

2 cups	wheat flour
1 cup	wheat germ
¼ cup	safflower oil
¼ cup	maple syrup
6 tablespoons	egg replacer
1 teaspoon	sea salt
2½ cups	oat milk
6 tablespoons	flax seed

Mix all the ingredients together. Heat a griddle, pour
3 tablespoons batter onto the griddle, and cook 3 minutes
each side, or until golden brown. Repeat until all the mixture
is used.

Oatmeal Pancakes
with Currants

Serves 4

1½ cups	oatmeal
½ cup	currants
1 tablespoon	hickory syrup
2½ cups	oat milk
	egg replacer for 1 egg
½ teaspoon	sea salt
1 cup	flour
1 teaspoon	cinnamon
1 tablespoon	baking powder
¼ cup	safflower oil

Soak the oatmeal and currants in the syrup and oat milk for 15 minutes. Sift together the egg replacer, salt, flour, cinnamon, and baking powder. Add to the oatmeal and mix well. Add the oil and allow the mixture to rest for 3 minutes. Pour enough batter to form one large pancake onto a griddle and cook until lightly browned, flipping once. Repeat with the remaining batter. Serve with more hickory syrup.

French Toast Feast

Serves 2–4

1 cup	multigrain milk
2 teaspoons	flour
1 tablespoon	yeast flakes
1 teaspoon	raw sugar
1 teaspoon	vanilla extract
½ teaspoon	salt
¼ teaspoon	nutmeg
6 slices	whole-wheat or sourdough bread
	safflower oil

Whisk together the first 7 ingredients. Dip the bread in the mixture, place on an oiled griddle, and cook until browned.

Want it stuffed? Mix 8 ounces of softened veggie cream cheese with choice of banana, strawberry, or orange marmalade. Spread a thick layer on one toast and top with another. Return to the griddle and heat until the center is soft and gooey. Garnish with fresh banana, strawberry, or orange slices.

Jeannie's Waffle Surprise

Serves 2 for brunch

1 cup	angel hair pasta, cooked and rinsed
½ cup	Red Sauce...for Pasta (page xx)
2	buckwheat waffles
2 slices	tomato
2 tablespoons	grated veggie Parmesan

Preheat the oven to 450°F.

Mix the pasta and pasta sauce and heat in the microwave 2 minutes, covered. Pop the waffles in the toaster and toast. Heap ½ cup pasta on each waffle, top with tomato, and sprinkle with cheese. Place under the broiler for 1 minute.

Waffles...in a Jiffy

Serves 4

2 cups	vegan waffle mix
4 tablespoons	egg replacer
4 tablespoons	vegetable oil
2 or more cups	multigrain milk
1½ cups	favorite diced fruit

Place waffle mix, egg replacer, and vegetable oil in a bowl. Mix well so that there are no lumps. Add enough milk to make a somewhat thin batter (too thick and your waffles will be dry). Fold in the fruit, reserving a little for a topping. Bake in a waffle maker until done, 8–9 minutes. Top with more fruit and, if you wish, dust with cinnamon or powdered sugar.

Ohmlette

Serves 2

12 ounces	firm tofu
½ cup	soymilk
3 teaspoons	chopped fresh parsley
2	garlic cloves, minced
3 teaspoons	diced red bell pepper
3 teaspoons	diced yellow onion, parboiled
3 teaspoons	diced celery, parboiled
½ teaspoon	turmeric
½ teaspoon	paprika
½ teaspoon	black pepper
¼ teaspoon	red-pepper flakes
1 teaspoon	sea salt
4 tablespoons	tamari
2 tablespoons	safflower oil
2 cups	sliced mushrooms

Place all the ingredients, except the oil and mushrooms, in a food processor and process. Heat the oil in a skillet and add the processed mixture. Cook on medium to high heat for 10 minutes. Add the mushrooms and fold the tofu over, pressing together and covering the mushrooms. Cook an additional 8 minutes.

Serve with World's Best Veggie Gravy (page 321).

Scrambled Tofu

Serves 2

12 ounces	firm tofu
3 teaspoons	chopped fresh parsley
2	garlic cloves, minced
3 teaspoons	diced red bell pepper
3 teaspoons	diced yellow onion, parboiled
½	baked potato, diced, skin and all
3 teaspoons	diced celery, parboiled
½ teaspoon	turmeric
½ teaspoon	paprika
½ teaspoon	black pepper
¼ teaspoon	red-pepper flakes
1 teaspoon	sea salt
3 tablespoons	tamari
2 tablespoons	safflower oil

Using a fork, crumble the tofu. Combine all the ingredients, except the oil. Heat the oil in a skillet and add the tofu. Fry on medium to high heat for 3–5 minutes, or to desired consistency, stirring frequently.

For variety: Add ¼ cup veggie cheddar shreds during the last minute of cooking and serve immediately. Alternatively, fry ½ cup vegan soy hamburger and ½ teaspoon minced garlic in a tablespoon of oil, add to the tofu and cook together.

Sandwiches and Snacks:

HOT OR COLD VEGAN SPECIALS

FOR LUNCH OR ANY TIME!

Sandwiches and snacks make

on-the-go dining a fine art ...

filled with good fun and laughter!

California Wrap

Serves 4

4 tablespoons	wasabi paste
4 pinches	five-spice powder
4	large flour tortillas
1 cup	sticky rice
1	medium cucumber, peeled and diced
1 cup	daikon radish sprouts
1 cup	shredded carrot
1 cup	shredded red cabbage
2	avocados, peeled, sliced into wedges
4 teaspoons	tamari

Mix the wasabi with the five-spice powder and enough water to give the consistency of a thick sauce. Place the tortillas on a flat surface. Spread each tortilla with a tablespoon of wasabi sauce, then add ¼ cup of rice, a quarter of the cucumber, the sprouts, carrot, and cabbage. Place the avocado slices on top, sprinkle with a teaspoon of tamari; roll and cut in half.

Creole Poor Boys

Serves 4

1¼ cups	flour
½ teaspoon	powdered vegetable seasoning
½ teaspoon	pepper
2 teaspoons	creole seasoning
½ cup	veggie sour cream
2 pounds	veggie shrimp
¼ cup	vegetable margarine
2	garlic cloves, minced
4	French bread rolls, split
1 cup	vegan mayonnaise dressing
3	scallions, sliced very thin
2 teaspoons	creole mustard
1 tablespoon	chopped fresh parsley
1 teaspoon	horseradish
1 teaspoon	minced garlic
12	sun-dried tomatoes, chopped
1 cup	shredded iceberg lettuce

Mix the flour, vegetable seasoning, pepper, Creole seasoning, and sour cream. Dredge the "shrimps" in the mixture and fry in oil until lightly browned. Drain on paper towels.

Mix the margarine and garlic; spread on the bread rolls and place in the oven for 5 minutes, at 425°F, until warm and melted.

Mix the "mayo," scallions, mustard, parsley, horseradish, garlic, and sun-dried tomato.

Spread the rolls with the vegan mayonnaise mixture and follow with lettuce. Place the "shrimps" on top of the bed of lettuce and cover with other slice of bread.

El Hickory Veggie Torta

Serves 2

1	jalapeño chilli, peeled, seeded, and cut in half
½ cup	radicchio, roasted and shredded
½	green bell pepper, roasted and cut into strips
Juice of 1	lime
	hickory liquid smoke
1 cup	refried black beans
¼ cup	fresh cilantro, chopped
2 tablespoons	vegetable margarine
2	bolillo, both cut in half lengthwise
1	tomato, thinly sliced
Handful of	alfalfa sprouts
2 tablespoons	vegan mayonnaise dressing

Light the barbecue and roast the prepared veggies—chili, radicchio, and bell pepper, squirting them with limejuice and hickory liquid smoke.

Mix the beans with the cilantro.

Spread the margarine on the bolillos. place over the coals for 30 seconds then remove. Spread the beans on top of the bolillos, followed by roasted veggies, tomato, and sprouts. Spread "mayo" on the other half of bread and top the sandwich. Return to the barbecue and heat an additional minute.

Serve with Red Salsa (page 329) and Guacamole "Dressing" (page 303).

Falafel Pockets

Serves 12 (or 6 very hungry people!)

1 package	Fantastic Falafel Vegetarian Patty Mix
	olive oil for frying
1 cup	safflower oil
1	cucumber, peeled and chopped
1 cup	tahini paste
2 tablespoons	tamari
1	garlic clove, minced
¼ cup	white wine vinegar
1 tablespoon	fresh dill, chopped
Dash of	pepper
6	whole-wheat pita pockets
3 cups	shredded iceberg lettuce
2 cups	shredded raw beets

Prepare the falafel according to package directions; fry in olive oil. Pat dry on paper towels. Place the safflower oil, cucumber, tahini, tamari, garlic, vinegar, dill, and pepper in blender, and puree. Cut the pitas in half. Place a falafel patty in each pita and top with lettuce and beets. Serve warm with the cucumber dressing on the side.

Grilled Cheese Sandwich

Serves 2

8 teaspoons	vegetable margarine
4 slices	whole-wheat bread
1 teaspoon	powdered vegetable seasoning
4 slices	veggie cheddar cheese

Heat a skillet, add 4 teaspoons of the margarine, and melt.

Spread 1 teaspoon of margarine on each slice of bread. Sprinkle the seasoning over the bread slices and place two slices of cheese in between the two sandwiches. Place in a skillet and fry 2 minutes each side, or until browned and cheese is bubbly.

If you wish, add a dill pickle.

Kielbasa Burger

Serves 2

2 tablespoons	diced onion
1 tablespoon	vegetable margarine
1 teaspoon	minced fresh sage
4 tablespoons	vegan mayonnaise dressing
2	veggie kielbasa
2	potato buns
2 tablespoons	roasted, chopped red peppers
2	collard leaves, steamed

In a skillet, sauté the onion in the margarine. Add the sage. Mix with the "mayo" and reserve.

Warm the "sausage" in the same skillet, adding a tablespoon of water. Reserve.

Warm the buns in the same skillet, then add the red peppers and collard leaves. Remove and reserve.

To assemble the burgers: Spread the onions on the bun then roll the sausage and red peppers in the collard leaf and place in the bun.

...Lettuce, Tomato—I Beg Your Pardon...BLT NOT!

Serves 2

2 cups	shredded cabbage
4 teaspoons	lemon juice
½ teaspoon	sea salt
1 tablespoon	hickory syrup
¼ teaspoon	red pepper
4 slices	veggie bacon
1 tablespoon	minced red onion
1 teaspoon	olive oil
4 slices	whole-wheat bread
2 tablespoons	vegan mayonnaise dressing
2 slices	tomato

In a mixing bowl, combine the cabbage, lemon juice, salt, syrup, and red pepper.

In a skillet, fry the bacon and onion in the oil. Pat dry.

Toast the bread and spread the "mayo" on the slices. Top with the cabbage, "bacon," and tomato. Outstanding!

Macro Wrap

Serves 2

¼	small red onion, chopped
1	tomato, chopped
¼	green bell pepper, chopped
1	carrot, shredded
2 cups	cooked brown rice
1 cup	cooked black beans
2	red-leaf lettuce leaves
2	whole-wheat tortillas
¼ cup	Savory Gravy (page 320)

Place the onion, tomato, bell pepper, and carrot in a microwave bag with 1 teaspoon water; microwave 2 minutes. Fold into the rice. Place a lettuce leaf on each tortilla, cover with the rice mixture and then the beans. Add the Savory Gravy, and fold.

Mediterranean Wrap 1

Serves 4

2 cups	hummus
4	large flour tortillas
¼ cup	diced celery
¼ cup	diced tomatoes
¼ cup	diced cucumber
¼ cup	shredded raw beets
¼ cup	shredded carrots
½ cup	alfalfa sprouts

Spread ½ cup hummus on each tortilla. Follow with the diced vegetables. Layer the shredded beets and carrots on top and finish with the sprouts. Roll and cut in half.

Mediterranean Wrap 2

Serves 4

4	large flour tortillas
1 cup	hummus
¼ cup	diced tomatoes
1 cup	Beggar's Caviar (page 333), warmed
1 cup	shredded lettuce of your choice

Lay out the tortillas and spread with the hummus. Follow with the tomatoes and eggplant. Top with lettuce, roll up, and cut in half.

Serve with Greek olives.

Monty Cristo 2000

Serves 2

8 teaspoons	vegetable margarine
1 teaspoon	finely chopped fresh parsley
4 slices	sourdough bread
1 teaspoon	powdered vegetable seasoning
4 slices	veggie provolone cheese
4 slices	veggie turkey slices
4	cherry tomatoes
4	toothpicks

Melt 4 teaspoon of the margarine in a skillet and add the parsley.

Spread the bread slices on one side with the remaining margarine. On two of the slices, sprinkle some seasoning then add one slice of cheese followed by two slices of turkey, followed another cheese slice. Top with the remaining bread slices and press together.

Fry for 2 minutes, turn over, and fry 2 minutes more—the sandwich should be lightly browned and the cheese bubbly. Cut the sandwiches in half and skewer a cherry tomato on a toothpick in each half.

Philly Cheesesteak (...Not!) Wrap

Serves 4

1 teaspoon	oil
½ cup	diced red, yellow, and green bell pepper
½ cup	diced white mushrooms
Dash of	powdered vegetable seasoning
2 cups	baby spinach
2 teaspoons	lemon juice
8 tablespoons	veggie cream cheese
2 tablespoons	diced red onion, sautéed
4	large flour tortillas
1 cup	alfalfa sprouts

Heat the oil in a skillet, add the vegetable seasoning, pepper, and mushrooms; sauté. Toss the spinach with lemon juice.

Mix the "cream cheese" with the onion and spread about 2 teaspoon over each tortilla. Follow with spinach, peppers, and mushrooms, then the sprouts. Roll and cut in half.

Great with Garlic Roasted Potatoes or Old-World Roasted Sweet Potatoes (pages 205 and 212).

Pizza! Pizza!

Serves 4

1	pizza crust
3 teaspoons	olive oil
½ cup	tomato sauce with basil
½ cup	hummus
¼ cup	diced eggplant
¼ cup	chopped white onion
¼ cup	chopped Greek olives
¼ cup	chopped black olives
1 cup	diced tomatoes
3 tablespoons	capers
½ cup	diced pineapple
2 cups	veggie provolone cheese slices
1 tablespoon	red pepper

Preheat the oven to 425°F.

Roll out the pizza dough. Spread the oil on the dough. Mix the tomato sauce with the hummus and spread over the oil. Place the remaining ingredients on top, finishing with the "cheese" and a sprinkling of red pepper. Bake 20 minutes. Serve immediately.

Portobello Mushroom Sandwich

Serves 2

6 tablespoons	olive oil
1 teaspoon	red pepper
4 tablespoons	chopped fresh basil
3½ ounces	sliced portobello mushrooms
6 tablespoons	balsamic vinegar
4 slices	French bread
4 tablespoons	vegan mayonnaise dressing
1 tablespoon	chopped fresh Italian parsley
4 slices	veggie mozzarella cheese
2	romaine lettuce leaves, shredded
1	vine-ripened tomato, sliced

Heat the olive oil in a skillet. Add the red pepper, basil, and mushrooms; sauté. Add the balsamic vinegar. Remove the mushrooms and keep them warm. Place the bread in the pan and brown. Combine the "mayo" and parsley and spread on the French bread. Place the mushrooms, cheese, lettuce, and tomato on the bread. Serve warm.

Quick-Rise Bread Dough

Yields 1 pizza crust

4 cups	bread flour
2½ tablespoons	raw sugar
1¼ teaspoons	sea salt
1½ tablespoons	quick-rise yeast
2 cups	warm water

Combine the dry ingredients in a large bowl. Make a well in the middle of the bowl and pour in the water. Mix with your hands for 5 minutes. Cover and allow the dough to sit in a warm place for 1½ hours. Flour the counter surface, turn out the dough, flatten it, and roll out with a rolling pin.

Use for recipes calling for pizza crust, bread wraps, etc.

Rancho Scripps Patty Melt

Serves 2

2	veggie burger patties
4 slices	sourdough bread
8 teaspoons	vegetable margarine
4 slices	almond Jack cheese
2	scallions, trimmed and split in half
2 teaspoons	vegan mayonnaise dressing
4	black olives, 2 gherkin pickles and 2 toothpicks for garnish

Preheat broiler for 5 minutes. Place veggie burgers under broiler and cook 6 minutes, turning once. Spread the bread slices with the margarine then add a cheese slice. Place some onion on top. Place in the broiler and cook 3 minutes.

Assemble the melt: Spread some vegan mayo on each patty and place in between the bread slices. Pop the sandwiches back under the broiler until lightly browned, about 90 seconds. Skewer olive-pickle-olive on toothpicks and place in the melt.

Ruthie's Eggless Salad Sandwich

Serves 4

1 pound	firm tofu, rinsed
2 tablespoons	yellow miso
1 teaspoon	turmeric
1 teaspoon	curry powder
2 teaspoons	Dijon mustard
½ teaspoon	sea salt
½ cup	diced celery
¼ cup	diced red onion
¼ cup	diced black olives
8 slices	wheat bread
4	butterhead lettuce leaves
4	tomato slices

In a blender, mix the tofu, miso, and spices. Fold in the celery, onion, and olives.

Refrigerate for 1 hour. Serve on wheat bread with lettuce and tomato slices.

Scripps Veggie Pepper Steak Sandwich

Serves 2

2	veggie pepper steak patties
½ teaspoon	red pepper
2 teaspoons	orange juice
Juice of ½	lime
2	French bread rolls, spilt in half
2	poblano chilies, roasted, seeded, and peeled
2 teaspoons	olive oil
4 slices	veggie Jack cheese slices
2	escarole leaves

Heat the oil in a skillet, add the pepper steak patties and fry until browned. Add the red pepper and orange juice; sear.

Squeeze the limejuice over the rolls. Place the bread rolls under broiler at 450°F for 2 minutes.

Put the sandwiches together: Place one slice of "cheese" on each side of a roll. Place a pepper steak patty, lettuce, and chili in between the rolls and cheese.

This is especially good with a chilled imported beer.

Spicy Veggie Lamb Pockets

Serves 2 generously

2	whole-wheat pita pockets, cut in half
1 cup	veggie lamb
1	garlic clove, minced
2 tablespoons	horseradish
¼ cup	vegan mayonnaise dressing
1	tomato, chopped
2	scallions, chopped
1 teaspoon	chopped fresh parsley
½ cup	arugula, chopped
	salt and pepper
Handful of	alfalfa sprouts

In a skillet, heat the veggie lamb and garlic. Mix the horseradish with the vegan mayo.

Toss the tomato, scallion, parsley, and arugula. Spoon into the pita pockets. Mix the veggie lamb with the vegan mayo and season with salt and pepper to taste. Spoon on top of the salad mix in the pockets. Top with sprouts.

Sub-on-the-Pond Sandwich

Serves 4

½ cup	Japanese eggplant
8-ounce package	veggie pepperoni, chopped
8-ounce package	veggie salami, chopped
10-ounce package	veggie mozzarella, shredded
½ cup	olive oil
½ cup	red wine vinegar
1 teaspoon	chopped fresh basil
1 tablespoon	chopped fresh oregano
1 tablespoon	chopped fresh parsley
4 tablespoons	chopped black olives
¼	red, yellow, and green bell pepper, very finely chopped
1 teaspoon	red pepper
4	garlic cloves, minced
2	French baguettes, sliced in half
½ cup	quartered roma tomatoes
4	romaine lettuce leaves

Dice the eggplant very small and sauté in a little olive, along with some oregano, until browned and crisp. Pat dry on paper towels.

Mix the veggie meats and cheese, the oil, vinegar, herbs, olives, bell peppers, tomatoes, eggplant, red pepper, and garlic. Place the mixture on the bread slices. Add the romaine leaves. Close. Slice in half and serve at room temperature.

Tempeh Reuben Sandwich

Serves 4

3 teaspoons	olive oil
8 ounces	tempeh (4 x 2-ounce slices)
¼ cup	white mushrooms, sliced
1 cup	red onion, sliced into thin rings
6 teaspoons	liquid smoke
1¾ cups	sauerkraut
4 tablespoons	brown mustard
1 teaspoon	maple syrup
1 teaspoon	fresh dill
8 slices	rye bread
4 slices	veggie Swiss cheese
4 teaspoons	vegetable margarine, melted

Heat the oil in a skillet and add the tempeh, mushroom, and onion. Brown the tempeh and sauté the onion and mushroom. Add the liquid smoke and cook 3 minutes more. Reduce the heat and then add sauerkraut; continue to heat thoroughly.

Mix the mustard, syrup, and dill. *

Place the bread under a broiler or in a toaster oven and brown.**
Spread the mustard combination on the half the bread slices; add the tempeh, mushroom, onion, and sauerkraut. Top with the cheese slices and remaining slices of bread. Brush with margarine. Return to the broiler and cook until the cheese is melted and the bread is crispy, about 2 minutes.

* Or substitute Russian Dressing (4 tablespoons vegan mayonnaise dressing mixed with 1 tablespoon diced tomato, 1 teaspoon minced onion, 1 teaspoon minced parsley, ½ teaspoon diced celery, ¼ teaspoon dry mustard, 1 teaspoon multigrain milk, salt and pepper to taste).
* *Alternatively, cook sandwich in a skillet until brown.

TJ's Smoked Veggie Wrap

Serves 2

1 tablespoon	vegetable margarine
½ cup	shiitake mushrooms, thinly sliced
¼	red onion, thinly sliced into rings
1	small zucchini, sliced lengthwise very thin
2 tablespoons	liquid smoke
1	tomato, thinly sliced
2 teaspoons	tahini paste
¼ teaspoon	grated ginger root
2 teaspoons	maple syrup
Dash of	sea salt
½ teaspoon	red pepper
1	garlic clove, minced
2 tablespoons	vegan mayonnaise dressing
2	whole-wheat tortillas
1 cup	alfalfa sprouts

In a skillet, heat the margarine and sauté the mushrooms and onion. Once the onions are tender, place the zucchini on top and splash on the smoke. Once the squash is tender, add the tomato slices.

Mix together the tahini, ginger, syrup, salt, pepper; fold in with the veggies.

Mix the garlic with the "mayo." Spread on the tortillas. Place the veggies on the tortillas, top with the sprouts, and roll.

Western Calzone

Serves 4

1 quantity	Quick-Rise Bread Dough recipe (page 385)
½ cup	grated veggie Parmesan
	salt and pepper
2 cups	vegan soy hamburger
¼	white onion, minced
1	garlic clove, minced
12 slices	veggie provolone cheese
½ cup	roasted bell peppers
1 cup	Picnic Barbecue Sauce (page 314)
2 teaspoons	olive oil

Preheat the oven to 400°F.

Quarter and roll out the pizza dough on a floured surface. Sprinkle with the Parmesan cheese and salt and pepper to taste. Heat the oil in a skillet, add the hamburger crumbles, onion, and garlic. Cook until the crumbles are brown.

Place a layer of crumbles over the Parmesan, followed by the provolone, then the roasted peppers. Roll up the dough in a round, then tuck ends under and pinch to seal. Repeat, making three more calzones. Cut each pastry top diagonally three times to vent. Lightly oiled a cookie sheet and place the calzones on it. Brush them with the Picnic Barbecue Sauce and bake 30–35 minutes, or until brown.

Serve with rest of sauce. High ho, Silver away!

Not-So Wimpy Veggie Burgers

Serves 6

2 cups	bread crumbs
1 cup	brown rice
½ cup	grated carrot
¼ cup	diced bell pepper
¼ cup	diced onion
¼ cup	sliced mushrooms
1½ cups	tomato paste
1 cup	vegetable broth
4 tablespoons	tamari
3 tablespoons	powdered vegetable seasoning
1 tablespoon	pepper
½ cup	vegetable margarine
4 tablespoons	chopped fresh parsley
	egg replacer for 1 egg

Mix all the ingredients together, except the egg replacer. Adjust ingredients for individual taste/texture with seasonings and broth. Add the egg replacer and mix well. Form into 6 patties. (They freeze well.)

Barbecue, broil, or fry—whatever you prefer. Serve on whole-wheat buns with the works!

Not-So Wimpy Burgers Deluxe

Serves 6

2 quantities	Not-So Wimpy Veggie Burgers recipe (page 394)
3 cups	shredded veggie cheese
3 tablespoons	green peppercorns
½ teaspoon	Dijon mustard
2 tablespoons	white wine vinegar
	salt and pepper to taste
¼ cup	olive oil
6	whole-wheat buns

Form the veggie burger mix into 12 patties. Mold the veggie cheese into 6 slightly smaller patties. Place a veggie cheese patty on top of each veggie burger patty and top with another veggie burger patty. Mold the edges over, firmly encasing the cheese. Grill each patty until browned, about 3 minutes each side.

Meanwhile, grind the peppercorn in a food processor. Add the mustard, vinegar, and seasoning. Slowly add oil to processor, mixing on low.

Grill the buns. Remove from the heat, brush the buns with the peppercorn sauce, and place a burger on each bun.

Serve the "works" on the side—lettuce, sprouts, tomato, red onion rings etc.

Easy Tortilla Chips

Serves 6

4	x 6-inch corn tortillas, each cut into 6 wedges
	canola oil cooking spray
Juice of 2	limes
½ teaspoon	lime zest
¼ cup	fresh cilantro, minced

Preheat the oven to 350°F. Coat a cookie sheet and the wedges with the cooking spray. Place the wedges on the sheet and sprinkle with limejuice, zest, and cilantro. Bake for 10 minutes, or until browned and crisp.

Carameled Apples

Serves 4

4	large Pink Lady apples
	wooden sticks
½ cup	hickory syrup
1 cup	vegetable margarine
2 cups	brown sugar
1 teaspoon	sea salt
½ teaspoon	baking soda
1 teaspoon	vanilla extract

Skewer the apples on wooden sticks. Mix the syrup, margarine, brown sugar, and salt in saucepan; boil without stirring for 5 minutes. Remove from heat and stir in the baking soda and vanilla. Coat the apples with the mixture and place in the refrigerator to harden.

Carameled Popcorn

Serves 8

1 cup	vegetable margarine
2 cups	brown sugar
½ cup	hickory syrup
½ teaspoon	baking soda
1 teaspoon	vanilla extract
1 cup	popping corn, popped
1 cup	roasted peanuts
1 teaspoon	salt

Preheat the oven to 250°F.

Place the margarine, sugar, and syrup in a saucepan and boil for 6 minutes. Remove from the heat and stir in the baking soda and vanilla. Pour over the popped corn and peanuts, coating well. Place the popcorn on a cookie sheet and bake for 60 minutes, turning over every 15 minutes. Cool and sprinkle over the salt.

Root Rounds

Serves 8

½ cup	safflower oil
2 teaspoons	cumin
1 teaspoons	cayenne pepper
1 cup	freshcilantro, minced
1	garlic clove, minced
3 teaspoons	minced onion
½ cup	fresh parsley, minced
	salt to taste
3	yukon gold potatoes, thinly sliced
2	turnips, thinly sliced
2	sweet potatoes, thinly sliced
4	parsnips, thinly sliced
6	carrots, thinly sliced

Preheat oven to 450°F. Grease 3 cookie sheets with oil.

Mix the seasonings together and sprinkle half onto the cookie sheets. Place the vegetables on the sheets and sprinkle the remaining seasoning on top. Bake for 30 minutes, turning as needed to prevent burning—the rounds should be crisp and browned.

Wheat Pita Chip Triangles

Serves 4

4 teaspoons	vegetable margarine
2	garlic cloves, minced
¼ teaspoon	red pepper
4	pita breads

Mix the margarine, garlic, and red pepper. Spread in the pita breads. Cut each pita in half and then half twice more. Place in an oven for 7 minutes at 375°F.

Juice Bar:

JUICES, SMOOTHIES,

AND SHAKES...AND OTHER

DELIGHTFUL SURPRISES

Quench your thirst and find your karma

Apple Bobbin' Boosberry Slurpie

Serves 1

1 cup	blueberries
2	apples, cored and peeled

Juice then freeze until slushy.

Apple Pear Nectar

Serves 1

2	pears, stalk removed
½	lemon, peeled
3	apples, cored if you prefer but not peeled

Juice and consume. What a pair!

April's Frozen Café Latte

Serves 1

¼ cup	espresso
2 cups	almond milk
1 cup	non-dairy whipped topping
12	coffee beans
12	carob chips, melted

Blend the espresso and almond milk then fold in the whipped topping. Throw it in the freezer for an hour.

Grind the coffee beans very coarsely. Add the carob to coat. Refrigerate the remainder of that hour. Slush the latte in a tall glass and add the beans. Fold in with a straw.

Wired yet? Got to be wired to do all that housework!

Black Cherry Smoothie

Serves 1

20	cherries, pitted (reserve 1)
1 cup	iced almond milk
1 teaspoon	vanilla extract
½ cup	non-dairy whipped cream

Juice the cherries then blend with the milk and vanilla. Fold in the topping. Garnish with that reserved cherry. Sip. Take a deep breath. Exhale. Haaa. Yes.

Bonnie Lies Over the Ocean Smoothie

Serves 1

1	apple, cored if you prefer but not peeled
½ cup	blueberries
1	banana, peeled

Juice the apple and then blend with the blueberries and banana. Stick it in the freezer for 10 minutes. Pour into glass and start sing'n!

Carrot Shake Concoction

Serves 1

4	carrots
1½ cups	iced oat milk
1 teaspoon	maple syrup
½ cup	non-dairy whipped topping
Dash of	cinnamon
Dash of	nutmeg
1 teaspoon	shredded carrot

Juice the carrots then blend in the iced milk and maple syrup. Fold in the topping and spices and mix until smooth. Sprinkle with the carrot.

Grate ... man, great!

Christopher's Mango Sensation

Serves 1

1	pineapple, outer skin removed and flesh cut into chunks
1	apple, cored if you prefer but not peeled
1	mango, peeled and pitted

Juice the pineapple and apple. Blend the mango with the pineapple and apple juice.

Mighty Mango—it attacks the senses: Hear it, smell it, see it, taste it … feel it. Sensational!

Dena's Delight Smoothie

Serves 1

1	peach, pitted
8	strawberries
1	banana, peeled
½	mango, peeled

Place all the fruits in a blender and blend. Wanna do the treadmill? Go, baby, go.

Dick's Mighty Mango Libation

Serves 1

1	mango, peeled and pitted
2	apricots, pitted
1	banana, peeled
1 cup	iced almond milk
1 teaspoon	lemon zest
½ cup	non-dairy whipped topping

Blend all the ingredients and pour into a margarita glass dipped in lemon zest. Welcome to paradise.

Hendrix Thai Tea

Serves 2

5	green tea bags
4 cups	boiling water
¼ cup	hickory shagbark syrup
½ cup	almond milk

Steep the tea bags with the water and syrup for 15 minutes. Chill. Serve over the rocks in tall glasses. Add milk.

Jerry's Peanut Butter Cup Shake

Serves 1

1 cup	iced oat milk
3 tablespoons	crunchy peanut butter
4 tablespoons	carob chips, melted and cooled
½ cup	non-dairy whipped topping

To make the iced oat milk simply put the milk in the freezer one hour prior to making the shake.

Blend all the ingredients except a dollop of the topping. Put that dollop in your mouth then take a gulp of the shake. Reese's ... eat your heart out.

Julie's Tangerine Tango

Serves 2

12	tangerines, peeled
1	papaya, peeled
2	bananas, peeled

Juice the tangerines. Blend the papaya and bananas with the tangerine juice. Hey Wayne, wanna dance?

Ken's Mock Bloody Mary

Serves 1

6	tomatoes
3	celery ribs
1	jalapeño pepper, seeded
Dash of	cracked pepper

Juice the tomatoes, celery, and pepper. Add the cracked pepper and garnish with a celery leaf. No hangover with this one.

Kevin's Kiwi Quencher

Serves 1

1	lime, peeled
4	kiwifruit, peeled
1 cup	mineral water

Juice the lime and blend with the kiwifruit and water—kind of like walking through the rain forest ... tropical, cool, and refreshing.

Korinne's Kool Aid

Serves 1

1	large bunch green grapes
½	lime, peeled
10	strawberries
1	banana, peeled
1 cup	apple juice

Juice the grapes and lime then blend well with the remaining ingredients. Serve with crushed ice and a sprig of mint.

Yes, it does go well with vegetable sushi.

Lynn's Liver Dynatron

Serves 1

1 bunch	parsley
1	beet
1	celery rib
1	parsnip
2	carrots
1	tomato
4	romaine lettuce leaves
1 shot	of wheat grass

Juice all. Chug-a-lug. Wheat grass chaser. Mom always told you to eat your vegetables.

Mango Madness

Serves 1

1	mango, peeled and pitted
1	orange, peeled
½	lemon, peeled
½ teaspoon	cinnamon

Juice and serve over ice or mineral water.

McRae Magic Smoothie

Serves 1

1	apple, cored if you prefer but not peeled
½ cup	raspberries
1 cup	oat milk

Juice the apple then blend with the raspberries and milk. Can't take just one sip.

Mike's Mission:
Pina Colada Possible

Serves 1

½	pineapple, outer skin removed and flesh cut into chunks
1	coconut, milked and 3 tablespoons grated
1 teaspoon	rum extract
1 tablespoon	maple syrup
	shaved ice

Juice the pineapple. Blend the coconut. Mix the two and add the extract and syrup.

Shake with ice. Pour into one of those fancy glasses and throw in an umbrella or something. Impossible.

Naturally Nora Juice

Serves 2

1 tablespoon	fresh parsley
1	cucumber
2	celery ribs
1 bunch	spinach
2	carrots
1 teaspoon	wheat grass

Juice. Marvellous, simply marvellous.

Neapolitan Twist Shake

Serves 1

10	strawberries (reserve 1)
1 cup	non-dairy whipped topping
1 teaspoon	vanilla extract
2 teaspoons	maple syrup
1 cup	iced almond milk
2 teaspoon	carob chips, melted

Blend the strawberries and fold in ½ cup of the whipped topping; freeze 10 minutes.

Blend the vanilla, syrup, and milk; pop it in the freezer too. Combine the melted chips and remaining whipped topping. Yum. Layer the three mixtures in an extremely tall glass— vanilla, chocolate then strawberry. Neapoliton. Square container. Checkerboard. Right: Top with that last berry.

Nog!

Serves 6

2 cups	hazelnut milk
10 ounces	soft tofu
2 teaspoons	vanilla extract
½ cup	non-dairy whipped topping
¼ teaspoon	nutmeg
½ cup	bourbon (for extra zip!)

Blend all ... party hardy, happy holidays!

Orange Judy

Serves 1

3	oranges, peeled
1 teaspoon	wheat grass
1 cup	iced oat milk
½ cup	non-dairy whipped topping
2	dates
1 dash	of cinnamon

Juice the oranges then blend with the wheat grass, oat milk, and topping. Process the dates and add, along with the cinnamon. Blend well. Oh, my.

Peach Cooler

Serves 1

1	peach, pitted
1	orange, peeled
1 slice	of lime

Juice the peach and orange. Serve over ice or mineral water and garnish with the lime.

Pink Sangria

Serves 4

2	peaches, pitted
2	pears, stalks removed
3 cups	white Zinfandel wine
½	pineapple, outer skin removed and flesh cut into chunks
2 cups	crushed ice

Cut the peaches and pears into slices. Mix with the wine and leave to stand at room temperature 1 hour.

Juice the pineapple. Add to the wine mixture and chill. Serve over crushed ice.

If you wish, garnish with a pineapple slice.

Plum Papaya Perfection

Serves 1

½	papaya, peeled
1 cup	oat milk
2 teaspoons	hickory syrup
1	plum, pitted
½ cup	non-dairy whipped topping

Blend the papaya, milk, and syrup. Mince the plum and fold into the papaya along with the topping. Flavor packed and good for you. Yum.

Raspberry Lemon-Lime Smoothie

Serves 2

20	raspberries
1 cup	almond milk
2 cups	lemonade
½	lime, very thinly sliced

Process all the ingredients, except the lime, in a blender. Pour into chilled glasses and garnish with lime slices. Hey Tom, find that lemonade stand yet?

Red Sangria

Serves 4

1	orange, peeled
1	lime, peeled
1	lemon, peeled
3 cups	Pinot Noir
2 cups	crushed ice
1 cup	orange juice (3 oranges)

Slice the fruit and combine with the wine. Allow it to sit 1 hour. Add the cup of orange juice to the wine. Chill. Serve over crushed ice.

Rhubarb Julep

Serves 4

6 cups	rhubarb
3 cups	water
Juice of 1	orange
Juice of 1	lemon
½ cup	maple syrup
¼ cup	cane sugar

Cook the rhubarb in the water; once tender, remove the fruit and add the orange and lemon juice to the flavored water. Mix in the syrup and sugar. Heat to dissolve the sugar, stirring frequently. Remove from the heat and chill.

Pour the rhubarb juice into tall glasses, filling half way. Top off with ginger ale or lemon/lime-type soda. If you wish, garnish with mint or orange blossoms.

Strawberry Fields Smoothie

Serves 1

10	strawberries
1½ cups	almond milk
	mint to garnish

Place the fruit and milk in a blender and mix well. Garnish with mint.

The Fox Trot Smoothie for "Hudson"

Serves 1 (... very thirsty little boy!)

½	pineapple, outer skin removed and flesh cut into chunks
1	celery rib
3	carrots
½ cup	oat milk

Juice the pineapple, celery, and carrots and blend with the oat milk. Wowsa!

Tom's Tonic

Serves 1

1	orange, peeled
1	peach, pitted
1	banana, peeled

Juice the orange and blend the peach and banana together; combine. What a way to begin the day!

Vanilla Bean Dream Shake

Serves 1

Contents of 1	vanilla bean
2 cups	iced almond milk
1 teaspoon	corn syrup
½ cup	non-dairy whipped topping

Whip it. Whip it good. Who says vanilla is plain?

Vegan Feast Grand Slam

Serves 2

4	oranges, peeled
1	banana, peeled
4	dates, pitted
1	avocado, peeled and pitted

Juice the oranges and blend with the remaining ingredients. Great for breakfast—you'll hit a homerun every time!

Very Berry Smoothie

Serves 1

1	apple, cored if you prefer but not peeled
8	strawberries
½ cup	blueberries
1 cup	oat milk

Juice the apple. Blend the strawberries, blueberries, and milk. Mix together and pop into the freezer 1 minute. Berry-delicious!

Watermelon Ice

Serves 1

2 cups	watermelon balls
1	pear, stalk removed
1 cup	crushed ice
	mint to garnish

Juice the watermelon and pear. In a blender, add juice and ice; mix. Place in the freezer 3 minutes then serve. Garnish with mint.

White Sangria

Serves 4

3 cups	seedless green grapes, stems removed
2	red delicious apples, cored and thinly sliced
4 cups	white Zinfandel
1 cup	fresh apple juice (1 large apple)
1 cup	fresh pineapple juice (¼ small pineapple)
1 cup	ice cubes

Combine the fresh fruit with the wine and let sit for 1 hour. Add the juices and ice. Mix well and serve immediately.

Yes! Yes! Nectarine Smoothie

Serves 1

2	nectarines, pitted
1	guava, peeled

Juice and blend. Look out Broadway!

Resources

The *Easy Vegan* is intended as a transitioning cookbook for those folks that are vegetarian and on the journey toward veganism. It focuses on "veganizing" dishes and creating healthier, simple, yet satisfying meals that are easy and stress-free to prepare.

With so many new vegan food products on the market today, it has become much easier for people to make the leap. This is the good news, but remember: in general, processed foods should be limited in the diet—too many food additives! I recommend reading labels and—always, always!—everything in moderation!

Let's now discuss some of the ingredients that I have listed in this book.

Meat and Protein Substitutes

I have listed these as "veggie this" and "veggie that" ... mainly because the textures and flavorings in many of the products on the market are just so spot on, many carnivores don't believe that they are not the real deal. (And guess what? That is the whole idea toward starting the transition!)

Most of these substitutes are a blank palette just waiting to soak up the flavors in your recipes. The following substitutes are contained in the various products listed.

Tofu—silken, firm and extra firm soy cake. Use it in sauces, entrees and desserts. Tofu is a flavor sponge with zero cholesterol and saturated fat but high in iron, calcium and omega-3 fatty acids. Freeze tofu overnight, then wring all the water out and sear or bake for a "steak-like" consistency.

Tempeh—fermented soybean cake with lots of fiber and a nutty chew. Fry it with spice and make your own "bacos."

Seitan—"meaty"-textured wheat gluten that is full of protein. I love to prepare seitan by braising it in a good vegetable stock or wine for enhanced flavor.

Beans or legumes—lentils, beans and peas are full of protein, antioxidants and fiber. Use them in soups, stews, salads and more.

Faux meat products—available on the market and coined as beef, pork, chicken, burger, bacon, ham, turkey, sausage, mutton or lamb, kielbasa, chorizo, prawns, salmon, fish, crab, scallops, tuna, lobster, salami, pepperoni—you name it. These flavored, textured products usually contain one or more of the substitutes I have listed above. These are marketed specifically for folks transitioning or missing the meats they grew up with ... or, more importantly, those tastes and textures associated with happy memories of shared meals and family experiences. Some folks will never try these products because of what they represent—I totally understand this. But if these products help other people to join us vegans on the "other side" ... the more, the merrier I say! The following is a list of some of the resources for faux meats available today:

Amy's Kitchen, Inc. http://www.amys.com
This family-owned business makes and distributes over 30 different varieties of organic vegetarian and vegan frozen products made from fruits, vegetables and grains that are organically grown. These include pot pies, entrees, whole meals, burgers, pizzas, skillet meals, toaster pops, pocket sandwiches, burritos and snacks. Also makes vegetarian and vegan canned soups and chilis, as well as bottled pasta sauces.

P.O. Box 449
Petaluma, CA 94953
Phone: 707-578-7188
Email: amy@amyskitchen.net

Boca Burger, Inc. http://www.bocaburger.com
Makes a number of meatless products, such as burgers (one a
Vegan Original), ground beef substitute, breakfast links and
patties, meatless tenders and nuggets, and chicken substitutes.
Now owned by Kraft, which is part of Phillip Morris.

20 North Wacker Dr., Suite 1360
Chicago, IL 60606
Phone: 312-201-0300
E-mail: marketing@bocaburger.net

Cedarlane Natural Foods, Inc. http://www.cedarlanefoods.com
Producer of low-fat, frozen natural foods, including enchiladas,
pot pies, Asian Veggie Chik'n dinners, quesadillas, burritos,
stuffed focaccia, veggie wraps and more. Many of the dinners are
made with soy protein.

1135 E. Artesia Blvd.
Carson, CA 90746
Phone: 213-745-4255
Fax: 213-745-4253
E-mail: feedback@cedarlanefoods.com

El Burrito Mexican Food Products, Inc. http://www.elburrito.com
Manufactures vegetarian soy products using non-GMO soybeans.
Items include Soyrizo (meatless soy chorizo), SoyLoaf (meatless
meatloaf), SoySteak and SoyTaco.

14940 Don Julian Rd.
City of Industry, CA 91745
Phone: 800-933-7828
Fax: 626-369-6972
E-mail: elburrito@elburrito.com or info@elburrito.com

Elena's Food Specialties, Inc.
Under the name Nate's, this company manufactures vegetarian
meatballs in three flavors and rolled tacos in three flavors. Uses
organic flours and non-GMO beans.

405 Allerton Ave.
South San Francisco, CA 94080
Phone: 800-376-5368
Fax: 650-871-0502

The Field Roast Grain Meat Company http://www.fieldroast.com
Manufactures a unique vegetarian grain meat made from grains,
vegetables and legumes that can be sliced, grilled, ground or
minced. Products include Lentil Sage Loaf, Smoked Tomato Loaf,
Mushroom Onion Loaf and Sunflower Country-Style Cutlets.

1225 South Angelo St.
Seattle, WA 98108
Phone: 206-762-5961
E-mail: info@fieldroast.com

Galaxy Foods Company http://www.galaxyfoods.com
Markets a line of dairy alternative products made from soy.
Includes veggie slices, cream cheese, butter, ice cream, yogurt
and milk. Under the name Soyco Vegan, they make vegan sliced
cheese, grated parmesan, chunk cheese, sour cream and cream
cheese.

2441 Viscount Row
Orlando, FL 32809
Phone: 800-808-2325 or 407-855-5500
Fax: 407-855-7485
E-mail: contact on web site

Garden Protein International
Gardein is a wholesome animal- and dairy-free range of tasty,
plant-based foods with a meaty texture. It is made from soy,
wheat and pea proteins, vegetables and ancient grains (quinoa,
amaranth, millet and kamut).

200–12751 Vulcan Way
Richmond, BC
Canada V6V 3C8
Phone: (604) 278-7300
Fax: (604) 278-8238

Gardenburger http://www.gardenburger.com
Makes a variety of frozen, meatless entrees made from
vegetables, grains and seasonings. Now features more than 10
products that are vegan, such as Burgers, Meatless Riblets, Flame
Grilled Chik'n, Meatless Breakfast Sausage and Buffalo Chik'n
Wings.

1411 SW Morrison St., Suite 400
Portland, OR 97205
Phone: 503-205-1500
Fax: 503-205-1650
E-mail: acole@gardenburger.com

The Hain Celestial Group http://www.hain-celestial.co/brands.php

50 Charles Lindbergh Blvd.
Uniondale, NY 11553
Phone: 516-237-6200
Fax: 516-237-6240
E-mail: news@thehainfoodgroup.com

Yves Veggie Cuisine (part of the Hain Celestial Group)
Sells a variety of meatless, fat-free products, including veggie
dogs, burger patties, breakfast links, ground round and sliced
products. Almost everything they produce is vegan.

Health is Wealth Foods, Inc. http://www.healthiswealthfoods.com
Makes vegetarian chicken-free chicken, beef and bacon products,
such as Chicken-Free Nuggets, Patties and Buffalo Wings. Other
products include a variety of Munchies, Egg Rolls, Potstickers and
Dumplings, as well as some kosher products.

1051-A Sykes Lane
Williamstown, NJ 08094
Phone: 856-728-1998

Lightlife Foods, Inc. http://lightlife.com
Manufactures many vegan meat substitutes with no artificial
additives, including Gimme Lean Beef and Sausage, Savory
Seitan, Fakin Bacon, four kinds of tempeh, Smart Ground, Smart
Links, Smart Dogs, Smart Cutlets, Smart Deli Slices, Foney
Boloney, Pepperoni Sticks and Marinated Tempeh Grilles. Read
labels carefully—some items may have eggs and dairy. Now
owned by agribusiness conglomerate ConAgra.

153 Industrial Blvd.
Turner Falls, MA 01376
Phone: 800-SOY-EASY (769-3279)
E-mail: infor@lightlife.com

Mah Wah Healthy Vegetarian Food, Inc.
http://www.maywah@vegieword.com
Sells full assortment of mock meats, sea foods and vegan meat
alternatives.

213 Hester St.
New York, NY 10013

Beverly Hills Caviar http://www.beverlyhillscaviar.com/specialty-
seaweedcaviar/vegan-caviar/
This company also carries the real thing—seaweed caviar
companies tend to come and go. Makes Vegan Caviar, a seaweed
substitute that looks and tastes like the real thing.

Spice of Life Meatless Meats & Jerky http://www.Spice-Of-
Life.com
Creates meatless meats and jerky that are wheat free, gluten
free, salt free, cholesterol free, high in fiber and protein, and have
the look, taste and texture of a wide range of meats. Products
are made from defatted soy flour, Bragg Liquid Aminos,
sunflower oil and natural spices and are 100% vegan. Items are
not only for vegetarians but also for celiacs, diabetics, low-
sodium dieters and athletes who require additional protein.

Phone: 800-256-2253 or 818-909-0052

Trader Joe's http://www.traderjoes.com
Distributes numerous products that carry their own label, such as
canned beans, canned tomato products, sauces, instant soups,
cereals, peanut butter, dried fruits, nuts, snacks, tofu (some
organic), prepared salads and sandwiches and more. Found in
many retail stores throughout the country.

P.O. Box 3270
South Pasadena, CA 91030
Phone: 626-441-1177

Turtle Island Foods, Inc. http://www.tofurky.com
Famous for its Tofurky Dinners, this organization produces
Original Smoked and Tex Mex Super Burgers, Original, Peppered
and Hickory Smoked Deli Slices that are low fat and contain no
MSG or nitrates, and five types of tempeh: Veggie, Low Fat Millet,
Indonesian Style, Soy and Five Grain. The company also makes
Tofurky Jurky and a variety of sausages and super burgers. All of
their products are organic, natural and 100% vegan.

P.O. Box 176
Hood River, OR 97031
Phone: 800-508-8100
E-mail: info@tofurky.com

VEAT, Inc. http://www.veat.com
Precooked "heat and eat" soy-based meat alternatives with the
ultra-realistic, meat-like textures of chicken, turkey, beef, duck,
pork and fish. Products are all natural, with no preservatives,
MSG, additives or coloring. All vegetarian.

20318 Gramercy Place
Torrance, CA 90501
Phone: 888-321-VEAT (8328)
E-mail: eat@veat.com

VegeUSA LLC. http://www.vegeusa.com
Under the brand name Vegetarian Plus, this company offers
ready-to-eat, all-natural, meat-alternative chicken, beef, pork,
ham and fish. The products are all vegetarian, with no
preservatives, artificial coloring, MSG or additives.

4257 E. Live Oak Ave.
Arcadia, CA 91006
Phone: 888-772-VEGE (8343)
E-mail: mail@vegeusa.com

Vegi-Deli http://www.vegideli.com
Manufacturers Quick Stix pepperoni snacks, Vegi Jerky and Vegi-Deli Pepperoni. All products are kosher and vegan. Now owned by Green Options, which also markets products under the Now and Zen label.

384 Bel Marin Keys Blvd., #D
Novato, CA 94949
Phone: 888-473-8667
Fax: 415-282-9791

Wildwood Harvest Foods http://www.wildwoodnaturalfoods.com
Makes organic tofu, soymilk, probiotic soy smoothies, soy yogurt, baked tofu, tofu cutlets, smoked tofu, vegan slices, wild dogs and tofu veggie burgers (three of the four are vegan).

1560 Mansfield Ave.
Santa Cruz, CA 95062
Phone: 800-499-TOFU (8638)
E-mail: dougporter@wildwoodnaturalfoods.com

Worthington Foods http://www.morningstarfarms.com
Morningstar Farms: makes a variety of burgers, patties, breakfast links and corn and veggie dogs.

Worthington: includes frozen foods, dry burger alternative and canned vegetarian meat alternatives

Natural Touch: makes burgers, tuna substitute, patties, veggie franks, entree mixes and Roma coffee substitute. All have no artificial additives, flavors or colors and are made from all natural ingredients with minimum processing.

Non-Dairy Substitutes + Milk/Cheeses Products

I am going to break these down into three categories: milks, cheese products and egg replacements.

This is about taking the BIG leap. For vegetarians, it may be easy to cut out meat products, but then to forgo the cheese, milk and eggs? That can be tough! It is one thing to replace cow's milk for soy, but it is another to switch flax for eggs, as well as to miss out on a gooey, cheesy-topped pizza ...

Non-dairy milks—If one is lactose intolerant, this is a no-brainer, but you too can make the switch! Soy milks are richer in vitamin D and calcium and are cholesterol free. Try nut milks like almond, cashew and hazelnut flavors; these have fewer calories as well as a nutty good taste. Grain milks such as rice and oat are also excellent sources of calcium.

Pacific Foods http://www.pacificfoods.com
Makes a variety of non-dairy beverages from oats, multigrains, soy, rice, almonds and hazelnuts. Produces organic soups and broths, as well as organic teas, Herbal Chai and Chai Green Tea blends.

19480 SW 97th Ave.
Tualatin, OR 97062
Phone: 503-692-9666
E-mail: pfo@pacificfoods.com

Rice Dream http://www.tastethedream.com/
Gluten-free rice milk, almond and coconut beverage products, etc.

Silk Soy Milk http://silksoymilk.com/
Soy milk, almond milk, coconut milk and more.

Tempt Hemp Milk http://livingharvest.com/products/
Hemp seeds are the edible part of the hemp plant (*cannabis sativa L*). Some may be surprised to learn that they are one of the best sources of easily digestible, high-quality protein. Rich in all 10 essential amino acids, the building blocks of protein, hemp helps develop lean body mass and promotes muscular repair. It is an awesome source of Omega-3 and Omega-6 essential fatty acids, which support energy production, nervous system function, brain development, heart health and a healthy immune system.

Westbrae Natural Foods http://www.westbrae.com
Markets a number of soy products, including miso, soy sauce, tamari and soy drinks.

P.O. Box 48006
Gardena, CA 90248
Phone: 310-886-8200

Cheese products—Cheese by the block, shredded, grated ... butter, mayonnaise dressings, cream and cottage-style cheese, sour cream, whipped cream topping, yogurts, ice creams ... all the dairy stuff that you can't live without or thought you'd never enjoy again. Until now. Years ago, many cheese products on the market couldn't hold a candle to the real thing. But it has improved a lot in the alternative department—not everyone likes the same thing, but there are products out there for everyone these days. Pick your favorites:

Coconut milk—buy it by the can and add a little vanilla and ½ cup powdered sugar ... beat with a mixer—awesome whipped topping!

Daiya http://www.daiyafoods.com/
Non-dairy cheese shreds and by the block in mozzarella, cheddar and pepper jack flavors.

Earth Balance http://www.earthbalancenatural.com/
The butter alternative. Mayonnaise spreads, coconut spreads, buttersand shortenings. The closest alternative to butter there is.

Follow Your Heart http://www.followyourheart.com
Makes vegan mayonnaise under the name Vegenaise. The four varieties include original, grapeseed oil, expeller pressed and organic. All are egg free, dairy free, gluten free and wheat free. They also make a large selection of natural salad dressings. They market Vegan Gourmet Cheese Alternative in mozzarella, nacho and caraway jack flavors.

P.O. Box 9400
Canoga Park, CA 91309-0400
Phone: 818-347-9946
Fax: 818-348-1509
E-mail: info@FollowYourHeart.com

Mimic Cream http://mimiccreme.com/
Use it in sauces, gravies and desserts.

Sheese http://www.buteisland.com/
Nine flavors of non-dairy, gluten-free block and spreadable cheese, including edam, gouda, blue cheese and cheddar flavors, to mention a few.

Teese http://www.chicagosoydairy.com/teese_vegan_cheese/
Mozzarella and cheddar flavors, as well as nacho cheese.

Tofutti Brands, Inc. http://www.tofutti.com/btcc.shtml
Makes non-dairy frozen desserts and food products. Frozen
desserts include Cutie Pies, Teddy Fudge Pops, Sorbet Bars, Rock
'n' Roll Dessert Cake and more. Non-dairy food products include
Soy Lavash, non-dairy sour cream, cream cheese and blintzes. All
products are soy based, lactose free, cholesterol free and kosher-
friendly.

50 Jackson Dr.
Cranford, NJ 07016
Phone: 908-272-2400
Fax: 908-272-9492
E-mail: tofuttibrands@aol.com or tofutti@nac.net

WholeSoy & Co. http://www.wholesoyco.com
Makes Creamy Cultured Soy, a yogurt-like product line that
comes in 6-oz. and 24-oz. containers and is available in 11
flavors. Also markets yogurt-style cultured soy drinks from
certified organic soybeans. Products are creamy, dairy free and
come in four flavors: strawberry, apricot-mango, peach and
raspberry. A Lite Smoothies line is also available in three of the
same flavors (strawberry, peach, raspberry), as well as an
additional flavor, vanilla. Wholesoy also produces organic,
cultured frozen desserts that come in nine flavors. The newest
offering in their lineup is a cream-cheese-style soy spread
available in Original and Garlic & Herb. Products are vegan,
gluten free, and certified kosher.

353 Sacramento St., Suite 1120
San Francisco, CA 94111
Phone: 415-434-3020
Fax: 415-434-2003
E-mail: robin@wholesoyco.com

Egg replacements—eggs are used as emulsifiers and as binders
in recipes. I generally use ground flax seed (1 tablespoon to 3
tablespoons water) or the egg replacer recipe in this book. If I am

baking and have left-over applesauce or bananas, I use 2 tablespoons of either ingredient for each egg.

ENER-G Foods, Inc. http://www.ener-g.com
Makes a wide selection of baking products for the health-minded individual, including vegan, egg-free Egg Replacer, sorghum flour and sweet potato flour. Dairy-free products include SoyQuik Beverage and NutQuik Beverage. Produces a number of snack items that are vegan.

P.O. Box 84487
Seattle, WA 98124-5787
Phone: 800-331-5222

Sugar

Yes. It is best to stick with natural sweeteners and stay away from refined sugars and corn syrups. I do have recipes in this book calling for karo syrup. Remember what I said earlier? Everything in moderation. Don't eat desserts every day, or if you do, remember to balance out what you intake. Other healthier sweeteners that I have included in this book ...

Cane sugar—this is unprocessed sugar containing molasses, with larger crystals and brown-beige in color.

Maple or hickory syrups—very sweet and fewer calories than sugar. Use it instead of honey.

Agave syrup—another honey replacement, full of minerals and vitamins. Low glycemic index so it absorbs slowly into the bloodstream.

Stevia/Truvia—all natural, non gluten, low glycemic index and zero calories.

Other Products

Arrow root—this starch thickener works at a lower temperature, though it is more expensive than cornstarch.

Agar agar—derived from seaweed, this is vegan gelatin. Use the powder form.

Marshmallows—these can be tricky to make vegan. You can buy them at the following websites:

http://www.sweetandsara.com/
http://www.welovesoy.com/

Butterscotch chips—
http://store.veganessentials.com/vegan-butterscotch-baking-chips-by-liebers-p3422.aspx

Vegan caramels—
Allison's Gourmet http://www.allisonsgourmet.com
Offers scrumptious, vegan cookies and brownies, made with all organic ingredients. Flavors delivered fresh to your door include Classic Chocolate Chip Pecan, Cinnamon Snickerdoodle, Mint Chocolate Chip, Lemon Poppyseed and Heavenly Fudge Brownies. Will gift-wrap items.

Phone: 800-361-8292

Liquid smoke—
http://www.amazon.com/Colgin-Natural-Hickory-Liquid-Smoke/dp/B0005Z8NCM

Miso paste—this fermented soybean paste can be used in sauces, gravies and soups. Find it in grocery stores, Asian markets and natural food shops.

♣ ♣ ♣

On a closing note, make this cookbook your own journey. Dare to create and discover new foods and tastes and have fun as you go. And finally, some tips for easy, stress-free meals:

- ♣ Read each recipe beforehand
- ♣ Prepare by gathering all of your ingredients
- ♣ Chop, cut and measure your ingredients
- ♣ Get your pans ready
- ♣ Don't be afraid to make each recipe your own
- ♣ Invite family and friends
- ♣ Share

Index

439